Avoiding the Dodgeballs ...at Work

A Young Woman's Guide to Succeeding at a First Job

By E. Marie

D1369213

First Edition
Copyright © 2013 by E. Marie
All rights reserved.
ISBN: 1484033957
ISBN 13: 9781484033951
Library of Congress Control Number: 2013906880
CreateSpace Independent Publishing Platform
North Charleston, South Carolina
Published 2014

Summary: a career guidance book for women on how to succeed on a first job or a first supervisory position and handle potential work related issues.

Scenarios are from actual events; although some of the identifying details have been altered to protect anonymity.

For information about special bulk order purchases, sales promotions, fundraising, educational or institutional use, please contact E. Marie at: e.marie@notadisgruntleemployee.com.

For previews of upcoming books by E. Marie and more products by the author visit: www.avoidingthedodgeballs.com

Cover and internal design by E. Marie with collaboration with CreateSpace.com design team.

Clipart used by license permission – clipartof.com, iclipart.com, shutterstock.com, istock.com and 99designs.com

Printed in the United States of America

I dedicate my first publication to my parents,
Mr. Kenneth Dorsey Sr., and
Mrs. Marguerite Yolanda Dorsey (in memory).

Thank you for giving me life. I love you both!

Welcome to the Game of Dodgeball

Before You Start the Tournament
Page 9

Rules of Engagement
Page 35

Watch Out for Who's in Your "Blindside"
Page 51

Working for that – 'You're Fired' Guy
Page 59

Fine Tuning Your Own Issues
Page 75

Playing with Your Colleagues
Page 107

Dealing with Reckless Teammates
Page 119

Making Moves While Playing on the Inside
Page 139

Switching Positions
Page 153

Exiting the Game
Page 175

Epilogue
Page 183

Acknowledgments
Page 193

About the Author
Page 197

Index
Page 199

Bibliography
Page 200

Chapter 1

After spending more than twenty-five years in the work force in a variety of sectors— corporate, union, governmental, not–for-profit, family owned and women led businesses—I have discovered there is one recurring theme:

"It is what it is."

Until you're the boss with your own company, you have to play by **their** rules.

And, for you ladies who decide to enter this "tournament," there is a lot more to going to work than putting on your "game face." You need to figure out how to navigate the work environment without getting hit or "knocked out" by an unexpected dodgeball.

Dodgeballs are work related incidents that could catch you off guard and possibly throw your career off course. As in the game of dodgeball, new employees need to learn how to "duck, dip or dive" in order to avoid these unpleasant events.

Sooo, "Katie," you are fresh out of college and finally got your foot in the door. After issuing dozens of resumes, attending numerous interviews, answering questions from some low-level "idiot" employee and wanting to scream— "WOULD SOMEONE JUST HIRE ME PLEASE!!!" – someone finally did!

"I got a job, Mom!"

Chapter 2

Before you start your new job, meet the team you will work with:

The "Good,"
The "Bad" and
The "Downright Ooogly"

1. The **"Sideline Cheerleader or Ms. Know-it-all"**—always critiques others but never comes up with any bright ideas.
2. The **"Princess Lady Dee"**—too good for the rest of the team, "This work is beneath me."
3. The **"Stirley"**—stubborn—as a piece of gum stuck in carpet.
4. The **"Ms. America"**—seems to have the golden touch, takes all the credit and proudly touts: "It's all about me."
5. The **"Jaded One"**—can't teach her anything new.
6. The **"Best Friend"**—the person with connections but no experience, who never should have been hired.
7. The **"Amityville Anal Aggie"**—wants to nickel and dime you on everything you say or do.
8. The **"Insecure Insamella"**— "I am so afraid the new gal will become the new favorite, so I treat her awfully."
9. The **"Luggage Lu-Lu"**—unproductive with no plan on going anywhere in life, leaving you no choice but to deal with her.

10. The **"Ms. Get a Hobby, Get a Man and Get a Life"**—perhaps you could stay out of other people's business and stop judging.

11. The **"Boss with No Clothes"**—senior management whose office has a bad odor and everyone smells it but him or her. Employees complain about the issue and it is never properly addressed.

12. The **"Jealous Jeepers"**—the haters—also known as individuals who cannot stand someone else doing something great in his or her life, whether it's on the job or outside of it.

13. The **"My Daddy Is a Board Member"** or **"Related Party Transactions"**—family members or friends who "raise a ruckus," break the rules and take advantage of a connection to a superior, knowing the boss will not fire them. So everyone's stuck with them.

14. The **"I Am the Most Religious Person in the Building"**—but I am also the most hypocritical and judgmental.

15. The **"Mr. Weasel"**—runs to the boss to "tell on" employees while distorting the truth to make himself look better.

If you do not recognize any of these people, you are probably one of them!

All of the team members listed are a combination of several people you will meet over the years.

Some, you will observe in action. Some, you will directly bump heads with. Some, you will start off on the wrong foot with, but eventually have a better relationship with, or vice versa.

Some of these people are from horror stories your family, friends or significant others will complain about to you.

I am just giving you a heads up on these folks so that you are not too surprised when you find yourself in the line of fire of a dodgeball aimed your way.

You know what they say: "In order to avoid a war, you gotta prepare for it."

"Before You Start
the Tournament"

Chapter 3

Sooo, Katie, are you ready to go to work?

Katie: Yes! How should I dress?

Good question! Although you have the job, you are still on the interview.

Katie: Really?

Yes, really! You are interviewing for your next job, which will hopefully be a promotion within the company.

Not only that, but some of your coworkers are observing you. They are looking for any weaknesses, and some of them are wondering, "How did she get the position?"

So, Katie, what do you have in your closet?

Hopefully you have researched your field and have knowledge of how people at your office dress. If not, on the first day, dress conservatively or at least in business casual.

Katie: Conservatively? Business casual?

For the last four years you were probably wearing T-shirts, jeans, sweat or yoga pants to class. But, perhaps in at least one of your classes, a group presentation required students to dress up in business attire.

Most of the male students probably wore a white starched shirt with a suit and tie, while the female students probably wore a blouse and a skirt, or a two-piece suit with medium high heeled shoes.

This style of dressing is conservative: a suit jacket, a nice blouse and a matching skirt or dress slacks.

Conservative Dress:

Business casual dress requires that you wear basic, casual clothing—no jeans, no shorts, no gym shoes and no T-shirts. You need to look neat and not distracting.

Business Casual Dress:

Many companies have adopted the business casual dress code, which allows employees to work in a more relaxed environment.

If the company does not have a written dress code policy, observe your managers and senior level coworkers. Your goal is to have their position one day.

Business Casual and Conservative Dress:

These suggestions on how to dress may seem elementary, but believe me; I have seen all sorts of inappropriate dress over the years.

New, young employees have come in with hot pink short skirts, stains on their clothing and ripped jeans.

They have left tattoos uncovered on their necks, arms and legs, or left piercings in their noses, through their eyebrows, on their tongues and around the edges of their ears.

Most of the time, they wear these things because these entry level employees have not been informed of the proper dress codes for certain work environments.

Chapter 4

Katie: *What about my hair, make-up, and accessories?*

Okay, Katie, now that you have the job, **do not:**

- put the nose ring back in—you know, the one you took out for the interview;
- streak your hair blue—the color you covered up in dye for your school's job fair;
- wear double high heels (stacks)—the shoes you would wear when you go to the club; or
- apply over-the-top make-up and nail polish—the look you would use on a photo shoot for a fashion magazine cover.

Remember, you are in the work place. Certain clothing, shoes and make-up are meant to be worn at the gym, beach or night club.

"You mean I cannot come to work like this?"

Nope!

"Or this?"

NO!!
Umm hmm...., I see I have some work to do with you!

"Okay, how about this?"

Only if you attended the interview dressed in this manner and they still offered you the job. Otherwise, on the first day, dress in the same clothing style you wore on the interview.

Check out the landscape first, and see what is allowable. If the company allows "edgy" clothing, look into those employees' positions. People in certain positions can get away with different things.

A lot of companies are moving toward a more relaxed work environment, which usually allows more creativity in their dress code policies. In various industries, such dress codes are encouraged.

However, if you are working in a normal business environment, there are some items you should never wear—even on casual Fridays. Some examples of clothing you should never wear:

- "Daisy Duke" shorts,
- low-rider jeans that show your "crack in the behind" when you sit or bend down,
- halter or tube tops,
- mini dresses or skirts, or
- see-through tops or bottoms that reveal the color of your underwear.

Again, check out the landscape first and see what is allowable.

Katie: *What if my funds are limited and I will not receive my first check for at least two weeks?*

If you are on a tight budget, check the Internet to see if there are thrift stores or consignment shops located in your area. At these stores you can find some great buys at below-market prices.

Some of these stores have a business or career section. Shoes and clothing at these stores are usually in great condition. In some instances, they are free to low-income men and women.

Depending on the season, many retail stores may have last season's inventory on sale. You usually find these items at the rear of the store.

Chapter 5

So, Katie, did you see your workspace?

Katie: Yes, I have a cubicle along the wall next to the water cooler.

I hope it is not too distracting. As a newcomer, you may not always get the best seat in the house. For me and most employees, any seat with four walls and a door is fine with us.

Be aware, "ear hustlers" are in your midst.

Katie: Ear hustlers?

Yeah, attached cubicles have "ears." Since they are usually mid size wall units surrounding your desk, cubicles do not provide privacy when you are talking on the phone, discussing certain business or personal matters. Whenever possible, try to limit your personal calls to your lunch break.

At least it is a cubicle and you do not have to see everyone who passes by your desk, however. As you move up in the world, you will probably obtain better seating arrangements. For now, you are the new kid on the block, still "wet behind the ears." You're just happy to have a job.

So, Katie, have you invested in any tools for your new job?

Katie: Tools?

There are some basic office supplies and equipment that each new employee should have in his or her war chest. They may include these items:

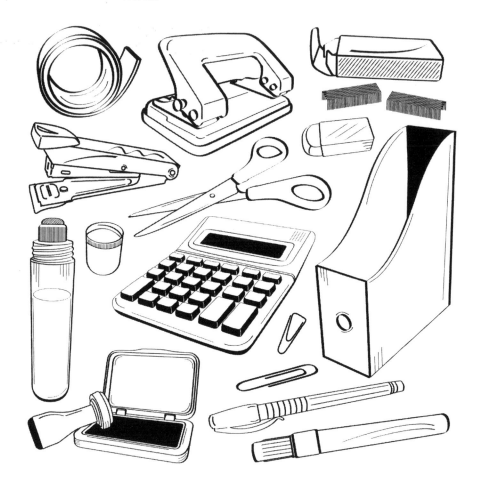

Cell/smart phone, iPad/tablet computer, calculator, laptop, note pads, pens, pencils, markers, Post-its, paper clips, scissors, stapler, ruler, Wite-out, calendar, glue stick, binders, binder clips, labels, file folders, desk organizer, in-baskets, envelopes and bulletin boards.

Katie: *Gee, will I need all of those items?*

Maybe not all, but I would not be surprised if you use most of these items by the end of your first year of employment.

The company might provide you with most of these office supplies. Your supervisor usually informs you in the interview about the cell phone and laptop requirements. If not, it's okay to ask about these things after the company offers you the position.

Chapter 6

So, Katie, do you have reliable transportation to get to and from work?

Hopefully, you have this issue worked out in advance. If you work in a big city, there are plenty modes of public transportation. Buses, monorails, subways or trains are usually at your service twenty-four hours per day. But if you work in the suburbs, you may need a car.

You might already have a car. If not, and you have decent credit, you could buy a new or used one. Some companies are associated with various credit unions that offer low down payments and interest rates. You might be able to purchase a car through your local credit union.

Katie: What are credit unions?

Credit unions are nonprofit entities—similar to banks—where employees can build up savings and borrow funds. Credit unions offer a variety of services besides car loans. Some services include: home or student loans, cashier's checks, savings bonds, safety deposit boxes and notary services.

Credit unions are usually member-owned. You must be a member of the credit union in order to use their services.

For company-owned credit unions, employees fill out the paperwork to borrow money or open an account at the company's credit union instead of getting forms from the bank.

It's usually easier to obtain a loan through a credit union because your repayment of the loan will come directly out of your payroll check.

You can check with your human resources department to see if the company is associated with a credit union. If not, you still can become a member by going directly to one of the local credit unions.

If you do not have a reliable car, you may want to consider carpooling. Check out your company's employee message boards or website and see if you can post an ad seeking a carpool group.

Carpools are great. It gives you a chance to meet someone from the company and get to know them in a setting away from work.

So, Katie, what is your start time?

On the first day, set in your mind that you will arrive to work at least thirty minutes to an hour early. Just in case you are delayed by a train or experience unexpected traffic jams, you have given yourself plenty of time to get to work on schedule.

If you arrive early, you can relax, read the newspaper, fix your face or hair, or drink some coffee. You will be surprised how many people show up late on the first day of work.

There are plenty of excuses for being late to work. Regardless of the excuse, being late on the first day is not a good way to start off with your new employer.

The weekend before your first day, drive your normal route or take different routes to see how long it takes to get to your destination in non-rush hour traffic.

You should also check the surrounding area to see where you should park your car or which bus stop you would need to exit.

Chapter 7

So, Katie, do you have children? If so, do you have reliable child care? Do you have a back-up plan in case there is a problem with your primary care provider?

As a young parent, it is sometimes hard to find a dependable baby sitter. You may start off with a great baby sitter and then, boom, something happens and you have to find a new child care provider.

Your boss will likely be considerate the first or second time you have to request a personal day off from work. If it happens on a regular basis, however, it may become an issue for you at work.

If you are new to the area, try to obtain references from friends and colleagues regarding day care centers and reliable baby sitters.

Try to build up your vacation and personal time as much as possible. When you need to take a day off no one should complain because you have the days available. Well, not everyone—there is always at least one knucklehead.

Katie: *Knuckleheads?*

We will talk about them later!

Many supervisors are parents, and you would think they would be considerate. However, if you are constantly taking days off without any accrued time, it will become a problem. When issues do arise, check with your supervisor to see if you can work from home.

With today's technology, you could set up a computer at home and link into the company's website to process work.

Depending on your position, you probably only need files you could save on a USB flash drive or memory stick.

If you are a great worker who regularly delivers on assignments, supervisors will work with you. When these instances occur, being a great team player will benefit you.

If you have demonstrated a willingness in the past to pitch in to help your colleagues, your boss and coworkers will step up and cover your assignments while you take care of the personal situation at home.

Chapter 8

So, Katie, are you going to sign up for any fringe benefits?

Katie: Of course. I need medical insurance and I look forward to taking vacation days.

Besides those normally offered benefits, companies have expanded their benefits to attract and retain great employees. When one becomes an executive level employee, you usually negotiate your benefit package.

Regarding free benefits—benefits given at no cost to employees—make sure you sign up for all of them, including fringe benefits you think you will not use any time soon.

If you did not ask about fringe benefits in your interview, the basic package usually includes:

- **Vacation days:** normally, ten days are accrued during or after your first year of employment.
- **Personal/Sick days:** normally, five to twelve days, used interchangeably, per employment year.
- **Paid Holidays:** ten to twelve days per year, usually including all federal holidays.
- **Health Insurance:** many companies pay a portion, usually fifty percent (or more), of the cost for single coverage. Ideal packages usually cover your spouse and children as well. High insurance costs have prevented many companies from offering such packages, however. Federal law requires

plans that provide coverage for dependants to extend coverage for adult children up to the age of twenty-six.

- **Life insurance:** many companies usually offer an average of $25,000 to $50,000 policies. Employees can purchase additional coverage at a cost to the employee.

Upgraded packages may include:
- Dental and optical insurance
- Short-term disability insurance
- Long-term disability insurance
- Long-term care insurance
- Pension plan
- 401K or 403B savings plan
- Transportation vouchers
- Tuition reimbursement
- Book fee reimbursements
- Scholarships for employees' children
- Employee bonuses
- Leased cars
- Extended vacation: three to five weeks of vacation instead of the standard two weeks.

Katie: *Wow, there are companies that offer all of these other benefits?*

Yes, maybe not all of them, it depends on the company's financial health and which benefits senior or executive management consider important to attract and retain valuable employees.

Chapter 9

If your company offers a 403B or 401K employee savings plan, sign up for it.

Katie: *What kind of savings plans are those?*

You can research more detailed information on the Internet or ask a recommended financial planner, but here's some general information:

Not-for-profits or certain tax exempt agencies offer employees 403B savings plans; while for-profits or private sector companies offer 401K saving plans to employees.

These savings plans allow employees to save a certain percentage of their wages free of income taxes. Employers usually withhold a flat amount per pay check. In these accounts, your savings grow tax free until you retire. Taxes are applied when you withdraw from the fund during your retirement.

Since your withdrawals are less than your annual salary, your withdrawals from the savings plan during retirement are usually taxed at a lower rate. These tax savings are another benefit to the employee. There are penalties for early withdrawals, however.

Some companies match their employee's contribution by a certain percentage, thus allowing employees to save even more. Most companies require the employee to work a minimum number of years before receiving matched funding.

Katie: *I'm young, and I have plenty of time to save for retirement.*

Katie, if you don't sign up for one of these savings plans, sign up for something. Even if you start off with just $25 withheld per paycheck, it's worth it. Think of it as another bill, except you are paying yourself. You won't miss it. Then, each year, increase the savings amount. Just like your regular bills tend to increase, so should your savings.

Katie: *I don't know. I hear all of this negative news about banks failing and the stock market going up and down. I'd rather put the money under my mattress, like my grandma.*

That's an option, but you also need to join some sort of formal savings plan. There is always some sort of risk involved with savings. Your mattress can catch on fire.

Most savings plans give you the option to choose conservative funds that are not too risky. As with anything, do your research first and follow-up with a recommended financial planner.

Chapter 10

By the way, after you are hired and have filled out personnel forms, Human Resources may inform you that you will need to make contributions.

Katie: *Contributions, to what?*

Some companies choose to support a certain charitable organization and will inform you that the contribution is on a voluntary basis.

The company will give you information about the charity and tell you what a wonderful job the charity is doing to help whatever cause they want you to support.

Human Resources will also tell you that the company is striving to obtain a reputation, with one hundred percent of employees contributing to this charity.

Would you like to give? Are you going to say, no?

Katie: *What's voluntary about that?*

Oh Katie, welcome to the working world!

In some cases, contributions will not be voluntary. It is part of the employment contract that requires you to give.

Katie: *But what if I want to give to another charity, such as my community day care center?*

You can do that. But Katie, you need to give to this one too.

This is one of those situations when you need to say, "It is what it is." Be a team player, sign up and move on to the next thing.

Usually the amount is not significant. You may not realize it at the time you are asked, but you will see that most contributions go to some great charities or are used to benefit your company. Anyway, your money may not be the only thing you will be asked to contribute.

Katie: *What else do they want from me?*

Your employer may also ask you to donate your time to charitable causes. Such events usually do not require a lot of time. You just hope it doesn't happen on a day you really need to be somewhere else.

If you cannot volunteer on a particular day, see if you can volunteer on another occasion.

Katie: *The interviewer did not mention these donations or volunteer requirements in the interview.*

It would have been nice, but they do not have to mention it. Besides, this item is not the only thing the company does not inform you.

By the way, did you tell them everything about yourself in the interview? Umm, hmm....Anyhow!!!

"Rules of Engagement"

Chapter 11

So, Katie, before you walk into the office on Monday morning, we need to go over a couple of rules.

Rule Number 2: Business is a sink or swim kind of world. So listen, be prepared to take plenty of notes, and don't be afraid to ask the "stupid" questions.

Usually in large companies, when you are hired, the agency probably needed to fill your position at least three weeks ago.

Due to budget constraints, many companies will not fill positions until they are hit with a major problem, such as a sudden opening, unexpected growth or legal obligations. When problems do occur, firms will hire new employees to prevent any more crises.

The company needed you yesterday, so you need to be up and running in a couple of days. Keep in your mind, everyone wants you to succeed...well most of them, anyway.

Katie: What about Rule Number 1?

Oh yeah, **Rule Number 1:** When it comes to your personal life, you have no best friends at work.

Young women fresh out of school, interns, entry level employees, read this statement **<u>again</u>:** you have no "best" friends at work. So stop discussing the juicy, soap opera details of your personal life with your coworkers.

When you are first hired you are friendly; you meet a lot of new faces and try to figure out who is really in charge. Along the way, you get comfortable with certain individuals.

You cannot come into the work place acting like a guest on the Jerry Springer show.

You do not have to come in guarded and stand-offish, but do not go around sharing all of your personal business. Save that drama for your girlfriends who do not work with you.

It's okay to tell lightweight information about your hobbies, children, parents and siblings. But, get to know your coworkers first.

Do not spill all the beans about yourself at once. Let them share. Feel them out first and let some of your personality come through by sharing some general information about yourself.

Coworkers do not need to know the following:

- *You love to drink, and you were "wasted" the night before your first day of work.*
- *You have to go to child support court during your lunch break.*
- *You filed an order of protection on your boyfriend's ex-girlfriend.*
- *You like to go on the boat to gamble.*
- *You and your spouse or partner, have a bizarre sex life.*
- *Your family does not like your significant other.*
- *You do not pay your bills on time, or you filed for bankruptcy.*
- *You have a sexually transmitted disease.*
- *You and your in-laws do not get along with each other.*
- *You like to smoke marijuana on the weekends.*
- *You had to bail out a friend or family member from jail.*
- *You think your spouse or partner is having an affair.*
- *Your mom had an affair on your dad, or vice versa.*
- *Your salary, religion or political affiliation.*

Do not become a "reality" TV show for your coworkers!

Chapter 12

So, Katie, are you married, dating, taking a break from relationships, or just "chillin"—waiting on the next person to come along?

Katie: *Uhh, why do you want to know?*

No reason, just curious about how you would answer. We will get back to that issue later under the office romance section.

Katie: *Oh, what about office romance? The guy in the computer department is kind of cute.*

Katie, proceed with caution and at your own risk.

I just have one question: If you have a nasty break-up with the computer guy, do you still want to see him at work every day? What if he gets a new girlfriend, and she is someone who works at the same company? Will you be able to handle their relationship? Will you still look forward to coming to work?

Katie: *That's four questions!*

Umm, hmm!! ....Anyhow! Let's move on. I have more important work-related issues to discuss. Besides, you can read the relationship advice column in your local newspaper.

Chapter 13

Although the hiring manager and the company want you to succeed, this desire may not be necessarily true of your coworkers. Not everyone is interested in your success, nor do they want you to come from behind and become the next "golden child."

Katie: *Golden child? What's a golden child?*

Every company has one—it could be you. Usually the golden child is a person who can do no wrong and is promoted swiftly through the ranks.

Most "golden kids" usually get along with everyone. Coworkers and staff from other departments tend to gravitate toward them for just about anything. Some golden kids earn their way up the corporate ladder, because they produce bright ideas that save or make a lot of money for the company.

Other golden kids move their way up because of connections that may benefit the company; for example, they might be the son or daughter of a client, benefactor or board member.

Some golden kids know how to work the system. They finesse their way to the top without taking any victims, while other golden kids or "goons" may step on other coworkers along the way.

Stay clear of the "golden goons" as much as possible and do not share with them your negative personal or work-related stories.

And finally, if you happen to be at the right place at the right time, you might hit the jackpot and become a "golden child" purely because of circumstances. This opportunity may happen to you or a coworker.

Whatever you do, do not hate on these employees. Do not become a "jealous jeeper" (item twelve on the "Ooogly List"). If anything, you need to network with them. They made it. Now you need to figure out how to get to where you want to go.

Chapter 14

Rule number 3: Do not fly with the "Angry Birds."

Katie: _Angry Birds? That's not on the "Ooogly List."_

Yeah, I just thought of these folks.

You do not want to hang out with employees who are mad at the world. If they are mad at the world, they are mad at the company. I call them the "Angry Birds."

Katie: _Why are they angry?_

It could be a number of reasons.

- Angry—because you drive a nice car.
- Angry—because you have some special perks and fringe benefits.
- Angry—because you are paid a higher salary than them.
- Angry—because you live in an upscale neighborhood.
- Angry—because you take nice vacations.
- Angry—because you wear trendy hairstyles and clothing that compliment you.
- Angry—because you are in healthy relationships with your spouse, family and friends.
- Angry—because the boss likes you, and you are the "it" person.

Katie: _Wait a second, why are they angry at me? I just started working._

That is another reason for Angry Birds to be angry. You are the new kid on the block with bright ideas—the teacher's pet.

It's not you personally. You are the current target of their anger. In a couple of months, they will move on to someone else.

Nothing ever satisfies these folks. If you notice, they are rarely promoted, and they do not have anything positive to say about the company.

As I mentioned before, there are no best friends at work when it comes to your personal life, but you will meet coworkers who will become your acquaintances.

Try to hang out with coworkers who have a positive attitude about their work and the company. You want to hang out with folks who look forward to growing both personally and professionally.

Also, do not evolve into an "Angry Bird" yourself. As you work in various companies or departments, you will see that things are not always going to be fair.

It could be your perception, but it will become your reality. You do not want to become stuck in the same place because you cannot figure out how to make things work to your advantage.

Do not discuss your coworkers' issues with other staff. Stay out of it. If they wish to talk about their issues to you, listen and try to respond in a positive or sympathetic manner.

However, you need to let them handle it. If you have a similar problem with this same person, do not speak ill of the person in question.

As they say, friends are in your life for different seasons; so are your coworkers. You could be working smoothly with them today, but next week you could be bumping heads with them.

You do not want these same coworkers who are no longer your acquaintances to share negative information you mentioned about other coworkers. If you share it with them, they will share it with others.

Again, figure out the landscape. Find out who's who. Know when to keep your mouth closed and when to shrug certain things off. Do not complain about your coworkers or boss to other staff or consultants.

Pay attention to what you do or say in front of others. Remember you may have "weasels" in your midst, and if an opportunity presents itself those weasels will use it against you.

Weasels will report the most mundane comments you may have said in passing. You will eventually notice that certain negative information about you is reported but somehow information about them or their friends, is not.

Chapter 15

Katie: When I worked as an intern last summer I didn't meet or observe any of this kind of behavior from my coworkers.

In fact, the employees I met through the internship were nice to me and I learned a great deal of information from them.

I do not doubt that your supervisor and/or coworkers were nice. Not all work environments are going to be as I described. However, the key words here are "internship" and "summer."

Internships are mentoring programs for high school or college students. Through internships, students gain hands-on knowledge about an industry they hope to work in someday. Throughout the internship, supervisors and coworkers actively mentor the students.

Students are assigned to experienced staff who will show them the ropes and give them insight into what it's like to work in this particular field, company and position.

During an internship, a mentor will delegate several projects to the student. On these projects supervisors will:

- give guidance,
- point out potential problems beforehand, and/or
- give immediate feedback on completed assignments.

Supervisors do this with the goal of ensuring the projects are successful.

Interns usually assist their mentors on large or small projects. Many of the tasks assigned to the interns may require research, reconciliation and/or data entry type work.

This work may be tedious to their mentors, but the interns will gain useful skills and valuable knowledge while completing the tasks.

Again, interns are assisting their supervisors. The work interns perform usually reduces the mentor's time to complete the whole project.

Therefore, the mentor appreciates the assistance. Because of this, supervisors will take time to answer questions and give as much guidance as necessary. Since they are mentors, supervisors want students to succeed and enjoy their time at the company.

Given that interns are in an apprentice or assistant roles, the pressure is not as great on them. A good mentor realizes interns are students and will take it easy on them regarding the production of their work.

As interns work on assignments, mentors will give them tips on how to improve their work. They will normally have plenty of patience; interns are not exactly working in a sink or swim environment. In some cases, mentors are also looking to impress interns with their own knowledge.

The company usually hires the intern at a fraction of the cost to hire someone at the market rate. In some cases, interns may be working for free to gain experience and knowledge.

Katie: *Why wouldn't they continue to mentor me once I'm hired as a full time employee?*

Listen, the company is now paying you a full-time salary. You need to understand that the safety nets are gone.

Your boss and your coworkers do not have time to hold your hand. Besides, some of your coworkers, who might be aware of your salary, are jealous. They are thinking, "Why should I help her? Let her earn her keep."

Now, the other key word is "summer."

The length of time for an internship is usually several weeks to a couple of months. During that period, time usually goes by quickly. It is usually a fun and exciting time for the student.

Interns are acquiring real life, on-the-job skills. They may not be aware of the subtle drama developing around them.

Also, interns are temporary guests in the employee's midst, and most of the employees are on their best behavior around them, including the boss. Well at least, when interns are present, most employees are acting like they have some sense.

Every now and then, an employee may slip and an intern may notice it. For the most part, the intern is immune to the drama and is into learning about the company and the new job.

Since internships last for only a short period of time, students are not there long enough to experience the office politics they studied in business administration classes.

So, enjoy your time as an intern.

As a new employee, bosses might give you assignments that will require a lot of grunt work and working overtime. You will work your brains, as if you were studying for a final exam.

Hopefully, you will get an intern to assist you.

"Watch Out for Who's in Your Blindside"

Chapter 16

In your first year, you are the rookie and you might get hazed. People you expect to help you may set you up, and people who you think will set you up will actually help you. Trying to figure out who's who will come with experience.

Trust your initial instincts and try not to be taken on too many "elevator rides."

Katie: *Elevator rides?*

Several times in your life, whether it is at work or play, you will be taken on one.

I remember having to attend a staff meeting at one of my city's notorious public housing developments. This meeting occurred during the time the city was tearing down the buildings. The gangs were fighting over territory that included a building that housed one of the agency's childcare centers.

It was a scary time for the residents, childcare staff and newcomers who worked downtown at the central office. Every now and then, we attended meetings in the community and one of the meetings was held at this childcare center.

As I approached the building, I tried to figure out how to get to the office on the second floor. The building was more than ten stories high. I did not immediately see an elevator and I did not want to walk up the poorly lit stairwell.

As I walked closer to the building, I saw two young ladies walking toward me. I asked them, "Is there an elevator that can take me to the second floor?"

They looked at each other, smiled and replied, "Yes," and pointed in the direction of the elevator.

I stepped onto the elevator alone and pushed the second floor button. The elevator went up past the second floor and then past the third floor, before it finally stopped on the fourth floor. The door flew open to a group of young men socializing in front of the elevator.

I reluctantly walked out of the elevator, startled and immediately asked, "How do I get to the second floor?" They laughed and said, "The elevator never stops on the second or third floors."

One of the guys in the group stood up and walked to the darkened stairwell and said, "Come, I'll take you to the office."

And he did. The individual, who I thought I might be afraid of, actually helped me. The person, who I thought would help me, actually played a joke on me.

I did experience a bad vibe when the young ladies smiled at each other. I should have trusted my initial instincts and asked one or two other residents.

At work, some coworkers will do the same thing. They may tell you the truth, but not everything you need to know. Do not get taken on the "elevator ride." Trust your initial instincts and ask additional, necessary questions about your assignments.

However, do not expect your coworkers to spoon feed you on every task. For some projects, you need to research on your own and not rely on the same individuals.

It is okay to think outside the box and ask others. You can also make some inquiries on various websites. Using various Internet search engines, you can find information on just about every topic. Taking these proactive steps will prevent you from asking too many "stupid questions" of your coworkers.

Chapter 17

Sooo, Katie, do you still want to go to work?

Katie: I don't know...the way you are writing—Angry Birds, elevator rides, and all...

Oh, you'll be okay. You made it through high school, pimples, boys and the mean girls.

For those of us who choose to go this route—"the Ninety-Niners"—going to work for others is not a "step down"; it's a means to an end. Therefore, it's a "step-up."

Remember, you and the company both have a need and something to offer.

The company's need is the talent and skills you offer, which helps them make a profit. Your need is a job, which the company will offer to help you make a living.

You need a job and the company needs an employee. It should be a win-win situation for both of you. The minute it becomes something else, you or the company will need to re-evaluate the partnership. Great companies do not want to waste money on bad employees.

So, just as you are seeking an ideal job that pays handsomely, the company is seeking an ideal employee who works exceptionally. But they cannot choose just any employee. It has to be someone who will work amicably within their environment. Therefore, you need to learn the ropes of working within the peculiar culture of the organization.

Katie: *Peculiar?*

Yes, peculiar! Each agency has different work environments. You have to figure out how to fit in and make it work for you.

What I mean by different, is each company or agency has some bizarre unwritten rules or policies. You will learn about unofficial rules—through gossip or word of mouth—or by breaking one of these rules unknowingly.

Katie: *Now that's not fair! How would I know?*

You can't, and it is not always going to be fair. The sooner you figure out this fact of life, the better you will be able to cope when you are confronted with unfairness.

You have to strike a balance, not settle: waltz with them until you get to where you want to be. It is an ongoing process, so be sure to set some professional and personal goals and make sure you are steadily moving toward them.

Chapter 18

So, Katie, we met some of the "bad" and "downright ooogly" folks. Now, let's meet some "good" folks.

Believe it or not, there are good folks at work. The mentors:

- There's "let-me-show-you-the-ropes" Amelia;
- There's "car-pool" Bob: if you listen closely on the drive to work, he will teach you lessons about life and more;
- There's "fun-in-the-sun, looking-good-for-a-sixty-year-old" Marie: she lightens the mood when things get tough around the office;
- There's "no-nonsense" Joe: he reminds you of a coach that ignores reporters' stupid questions. He will take you out of a bad situation and put you on the right path to success;
- There's "let me take you under my wings and 'push you' to do your best" John;
- There's "gives you public recognition for your good work" Al and Sue;
- There's "go on an adventure—travel to a new place for work" Raj;
- There's "setting the standards of how one should conduct herself in the face of conflict" Portia;
- There's "do what brings you joy and maintain some balance in your life" Brenda; and
- There's "let you have a seat at the table" Judy.

You see, there are plenty of good folks at work. It is not until you mature and have worked a couple of years with various supervisors, managers and coworkers, that you realize you had mentors all along.

Also, some of those bad folks were not really bad all along. You just hadn't figured out their issues and learned how to work with them, instead of constantly bumping heads with them.

At first, I thought I met my initial mentors after ten years on the job. As I look back, I realize I met them a lot sooner. You will meet your first mentor usually on your first job or assignment.

You are not always going to have visible mentors, however. Individuals who you think will help you will not always be mentors. Individuals who you think are not helping you may well be mentors.

Mentors will encourage you to do things you do not initially want or do not have the guts to do. They will help you see the bright lights. You may not realize it at first, but later you realize you have them to thank for steering you in the right direction.

Sooo, Katie, let's go to work.

"Working for that - 'You're Fired' Guy"

Chapter 19

So, Katie, what kind of boss do you work for?

Katie: I do not quite know yet. I am still trying to figure her out. One minute I think she requires the work to be presented in one way and the next minute it's something else.

Yeah, I know what you mean. One minute, you could be working for Mr. Dithers, next week you are reporting to the "Devil Wears Prada" lady.

Katie: Who's Mr. Dither's?

Brush up on your reading Katie. After you read this book, read the comics!

On any new job, you need to learn your supervisor, boss or manager's needs, managing styles and comfort zones.

Katie: Yes, but I thought I had some autonomy in completing my assignments.

Katie, there you go again, still in the mindset that the world is perfect—you still have a lot to learn.

Some bosses will tell you that they want you to complete an assignment in one particular manner. Later, when they review it, it's not what they want. Or, if you take the initiative to approach the work using one particular method, your supervisor might question why you went about it in that way.

It's like walking a puppy for the first time. Some managers give you plenty of rope to complete assignments. Others keep you close on a leash. It's a matter of their comfort zone and the amount of trust and confidence bosses have in you.

Trust: it's important.

You both need to feel each other out and the bottom line is, your boss has to trust you.

Other than the interview, background check and items listed on your resume, your boss really does not know you. At this point, you are no different than a stranger. Your boss could have met you on a dating website.

Before the boss can trust you with the keys to the building, the safe or the broom closet, he needs to have confidence you will:

- complete assignments,
- represent him and the company in a positive manner,
- keep information confidential, and
- have his back.

First, do not expect the boss to know all the little details of your assignment or a particular project. *That's your job to figure out.*

He will know the big picture and will give you guidance. But do not expect them to know how to perform each and every part of your assignment.

A good manager knows how to properly delegate work. So when he tells you that he cannot perform a relatively easy task, such as creating a simple spreadsheet, or does not know a basic software program, do not smirk and think, "How did he become a manager?"

Well he must have done something right because he is the boss and you report to him. Get this notion out of your mind; just because you know how to do something better than he, does not mean you are smarter than your boss. Besides, it is not how much you know, it's what you do with the information that you do know.

Every now and then, you do come across an idiot boss. Your boss is an idiot not because she or he does not know how to perform a particular task, rather, because she or he has a bad attitude. When they do not know something, the boss tries to blame you or someone else.

This occurrence is rare, so, for the most part, show respect to your boss. He has been in the position where you are currently working and paid his dues by working under other bosses. As a matter of fact, he is still working under other bosses.

Until you step into your supervisor's shoes, listen and learn how to be a good follower. If you are ambitious and seeking to move up to higher positions, your turn is coming.

I remember making a phone call to my former manager thanking him for being such a great supervisor and mentor. But I also found myself apologizing for not being more supportive to him in various situations.

Of course, I was in his position and I now knew what he already knew: supervising employees is like babysitting a bunch of kids. Each kid is different and has his or her unique, bratty issues.

Okay, not all. You will have at least one or two in the bunch who act responsibly. But every now and then, they too may fall off the wagon.

Some of those negative habits you had as a child usually carry over into adulthood. The difference is mom or dad is not here to nag you about it.

Bosses would rather spend their time figuring out how to get the work completed, instead of dealing with problem employees. If you want your boss to treat you like an adult, then you need to act like a responsible adult.

Chapter 20

Some people just simply cannot recite the words "I'm sorry." They cannot admit when they are wrong because they think it makes them look weak. These people may be your bosses or your coworkers. Do not become needy and always expect an apology from them. You won't get it. Work on yourself and develop some thick skin.

Katie: *Thick skin?*

Yeah, thick skin, or put on some padding. That is, work on your reactions and control your emotions when people throw darts at you.

You are going to have to be able to take the good and the bad. Bosses and coworkers—just like children—will throw some pretty powerful punches. When you receive one and fall down, you will need to learn how to bounce right back up.

When you start an entry level position, people do not start off being mean to you. Along the way, you may need some knee and elbow padding, though. As time moves on, and you move up the ladder, you may require extra equipment such as football pads to guard against your emotions.

Katie: *Okay if they are so smart, why do bosses use bad judgment and make such dumb decisions or no decisions?*

You make these comments because at your level of employment, you do not have the big picture.

Katie: *You keep mentioning those three words, what's the big picture?*

Oh, that? You will see this phrase often. The big picture is a phrase that Jim, one of my great bosses of the past, used to say in his meetings: "Let me share with you—the big picture."

From the boss's view it could mean several things:

- what is currently going on at the company,
- what direction we are taking the company, or,
- what objectives and goals the company is trying to accomplish in the next five years.

Katie: *So how does that phrase relate to the questionable decisions bosses make?*

At your level, you cannot see everything from the bottom that is actually going on at the top. Let me walk you through where you are now and where your supervisors or bosses are today.

Imagine that the picture below represents you and five of your colleagues. Katie, I know it's only three climbers, just work with me.

You guys and gals are new hires, just starting your careers in the workplace. You are still trying to figure out the dynamics of your position.

As you climb the ladder, you begin to notice certain staff or procedures seem out of place. You start to question—in your head or out loud—why certain aspects of the company are the way they are.

Such as:

- Why do we have to go to the basement to make copies? Why don't they purchase a small copier for each department?
- Why are we completing several forms to complete a specific task? Why don't they redesign the form to include all pertinent information on a single form?

These are questions you do not ask of your immediate supervisor. You think senior or executive management should already know to put copiers directly into departments or design an efficient form, right? Wrong!

Just as you cannot see everything from the bottom, bosses cannot see everything from the top. Depending on the size of the company, there could be many layers between the boss and you.

Bosses may already have a copier in their office and, therefore, they might not see the need for others to have one. Small changes, such as this one, would allow employees to work more efficiently with a greater output, which could lead to a larger profit margin.

Katie: *But still, why can't the bosses make these simple changes?*

Because, Katie, the bosses are not viewing things from your level. When these situations happen, item eleven on the "Ooogly List" occurs—"Bosses with no Clothes"—everyone sees there is a problem but the bosses.

Bosses are busy working on more important crises, such as:

- trying to prepare for an audit from the IRS;
- trying to refinance the mortgage on two office buildings;

- trying to prevent the city from closing a factory for building code violations;
- trying to oversee a major building renovation;
- trying to get a vendor to extend the company credit and ship supplies needed to complete the company's products;
- trying to prevent a competitor from stealing one of the company's major customers;
- trying to ward off a strike by union employees;
- trying to prevent a lawsuit from a former disgruntled employee or contractor;
- trying to increase enrollment to prevent a grant from being cancelled; or,
- trying to make payroll, or pay the light bill.

As you can see, there are a lot of things that might prevent your boss from seeing simple changes that would make the company more efficient.

Do not complain: instead, you can get on the path to becoming a "golden child" by making positive suggestions.

Remember, your suggestions need to have a benefit attached to them. Do not feel disheartened if your suggestions are not immediately received.

Some bosses and managers need time to let new ideas sink in with them. It's also possible your ideas cannot be implemented due to lack of funding or other priorities that need to be addressed first.

Chapter 21

In time, at least three of you folks will climb a couple of notches via promotions:

Katie: *What happened to the other three?*

Well, one of them may need a little more help moving up the ladder. He will eventually climb up, but at a slower pace.

As for the other two, one employee may have decided to leave the company for various reasons—like starting a new job or returning to school full time. The last guy or gal, depending on the position, enjoys working on his current projects and may not want to move into middle management.

Not all employees are cut out to be supervisors. However, they still grow by receiving interesting projects.

As you move up the ladder, you become more aware of the decision making process and have inside knowledge of what drives some decisions that bosses make.

Katie: *Okay, if the top bosses do not see the changes that need to be made, why doesn't my immediate supervisor make the changes? She always seems scared to ask for things.*

Oh, Katie, you are the "**emerald green**" employee. Wait until you step into your supervisor's shoes. Just like a newly elected politician, you will see it is not easy getting a simple, common sense law passed.

Look at all the political candidates who want to get into office. Year after year, they campaign against an incumbent mayor, governor or president. When these guys or gals get elected, they see it's no cakewalk. You have to get the buy-in from everyone just to put up a street sign.

Supervisors do not always have the autonomy you think they have. There are some changes supervisors could probably make on their own, without obtaining prior permission. It really depends on the management style of the executive staff and the organization's culture.

Some executive management teams run a centralized management system—all decisions have to go through them. Others run a decentralized management system—they delegate key tasks to capable folks to make important decisions.

Some supervisors may also have to obtain the buy-in from other supervisors or managers in order to implement new policies or procedures. It is not always as simple as it seems.

In the meantime, work on your craft and be a team player. Assist your supervisor in getting changes made that will benefit your work and do not pout if the changes are not made or are not made soon enough.

Now that you have a better picture of how things work, recognize supervisors or bosses are at the top, paving the way for you. Fresh ideas usually come from young or new employees.

You are in the "thinking outside the box" mode, the reason the bosses hired you. Your quirky ideas will assist them in reaching their goals and making the company profitable.

Eventually, bosses, managers or supervisors will either retire, get promoted or go on to new adventures at different companies. Their departure clears the path for you.

When you walk in their shoes, faced with the same challenges, hopefully you will seek input from your staff, including a new kid on the block, such as yourself.

"Fine Tuning Your Own Issues"

Chapter 22

So, Katie, let's work on you.

Katie: *Huh, what's wrong with me?*

As the newcomer, you could possess any, some, or all of these typical problems:

- I'm having trouble fitting into the work environment and I cannot get along with my coworkers.
- I think I am smarter than my boss or other employees.
- I always run to my boss when I have a problem.
- I allow others to speak to me in a condescending way.
- I only work on my projects and I do not assist others.
- I do not share important information.
- I am anal and I have to be told everything verbally. When I am told, I have the nerve to say, "I know that already."
- I am late on just about everything and I cannot manage my time.
- I rush through projects and do not thoroughly review my work.
- I have difficulty turning in travel or supply receipts.
- I have a grumpy disposition and I am not approachable.
- I am not flexible and I am always right.
- I cannot multi-task; I get "flustered."
- I am afraid to approach others about difficult issues.
- I have body odor or bad breath.

- I do not listen or I interrupt when others are speaking.
- I get defensive when someone points out a mistake and I blame others for my mistakes.
- I get an attitude when things do not go my way.

Some common themes here: employee needs to improve her communications skills, get organized, produce quality work, build self esteem and learn how to work in a team environment.

In other words: Work on yourself.

Most employees do not have all of these issues at once, but they usually possess one or several of these issues at some point.

Over time, your supervisor or coworkers will give you some hints about yourself and, hopefully, you will pick up on them.

We are human, and just like the bosses; we are oblivious to our own issues. It's not until someone points them out that we realize we have an issue. It's a work-in-process kind of thing. I am still working on some of mine.

So, Katie, do you think you possess any of these issues?

Katie: No! But some of those issues remind me of someone I used to date.

Good one, Katie!

If you don't see yourself on this list, your issue may not be on the list. Dig deep Katie, I'm sure you will come up with something. If not, that may be an issue itself. Yes, Katie you do have some issues.

Chapter 23

So, Katie, you are starting to feel comfortable in your position. Once the boss gives you a little more rope, do you take it?

Do not consistently ask your boss questions to which you already know the answer.

Katie: *What do you mean?*

If the bathroom door is clearly marked "women" on it, do not ask your boss, "Is it okay to go into this restroom instead of the door marked 'men'?"

Katie: *Why would I ask that question?*

Yeah, the answer seems obvious, right? Well, there are going to be some obvious decisions you need to make on your own at work.

Because you want to be careful not to make a mistake on an assignment, you might ask your boss questions first, before researching it on your own. Or, if you encounter something different within a task, you might ask your boss for guidance. You want to make sure it is okay to take a certain approach before you make a move on different tasks of the project.

Over time, constantly asking these types of questions or obtaining assurances will drive your boss crazy. Make a decision already, and move forward!

- If you are preparing a monthly report for the first time, look at last month's report to get an idea of how to complete it.

- If you never used a certain office machine such as a copier, play around with the keys; insert a test sheet of paper in the feeder and try it out.
- If someone has a question about a report prepared by someone other than you, review the report to see if you can locate the answer.
- If you are responsible for ordering food and your boss is in a meeting at noon and the meeting starts in fifteen minutes, serve the food.

Whatever you do, do not use the excuse, "I have never done it before."

Trust yourself and give it a try. Do not hold up the project because the boss is not available to answer your questions regarding decisions you can make on your own.

Katie: *How do I know I made the right decision?*

You won't. Not always, anyway.

If you can reason or validate in your head that this action is the correct option, then go with that decision. If it is indeed a mistake, give your justification to the boss.

He may be able to poke holes in your explanation. Remember, he is coming from a big picture point of view. Since your boss has more experience than you, he will immediately see the right action to take.

You will make some mistakes, but you will learn and grow from those mistakes. Shake it off and move on to the next project. The boss will hold your hand at the start of your employment. However, over time he will expect you to pick up and go with it.

Chapter 24

Then again, there are some employees, who are **way** on the other side of the spectrum.

Katie: Which employees?

The employee who never verifies data or thinks through decisions.

Katie: I thought you did not want us to ask questions, especially if we feel we have a good reason.

That's not what I wrote. Did I?

Katie: Yes, you did!

Okay, well this is what I meant: I do not want you to ask obvious questions you already know the answers to or can make a reasonable choice about.

At the same time, make sure you review your work, research your topic and analyze your decision before you jump in the lake. Make sure there is no underwater current lurking within your project. Unexpected problems could drag you under because you did not conduct proper research.

You can do the research without bogging down your boss with questions you need to research on your own. If you have too many mistakes, or pull your boss away with too many questions, it becomes time consuming. It's like the law of diminishing returns.

Katie: Diminishing what?

The boss begins to think, "I could have completed this task myself." That is, the boss could have completed the project on his own, in less time than he spent explaining and answering your questions. His investment of time on your portion of the assigned project should be minimal. Otherwise the work is not produced efficiently, which ultimately costs the company time and money.

Chapter 25

So, Katie, how is your baseball IQ?

Katie: Baseball IQ?

In little league baseball, for seven and eight year olds, coaches tend to draft kids who have a high baseball IQ. Like, if the ball comes your way, as the defender you are not afraid to catch it. You want the ball! Once you get the ball, you know what to do with the ball. You don't throw it away and let a player on the opposing team score on you.

In other words, you want baseball players on your team that play smart like Derek Jeter or Jalen Greer.

The same logic is at play in the work place. Bosses want team members who have a high work IQ. People who are not afraid of the project; who use common sense in making decisions about work.

There is a position for each team member, which position is yours? Not everyone can play shortstop, catcher, pitcher or outfield. Nor can everyone be the lead-off man.

Katie: Lead-off man?

Yeah, the team player that is going to get the project started. They are contact hitters and will get on first base ninety percent of the time.

The other team members will assist and help their team mates move around the bases and get the work done.

Katie: *Contact hitters? Bases? Shortstop? I'm sorry; I have not watched any baseball games lately. I have heard of that Derek Jeter guy, but who's Jalen Greer?*

Oh, just someone you will come to know in the future. No need to Google him—yet.

Okay, let me explain it another way.

The pitcher on the team throws the ball to the hitter. As the pitcher on a team, you have to be able to throw the ball accurately across the plate. As the pitcher on a specific project at work, you need to be able to perform a specific skill other coworkers on the team may not be able to perform.

You might be the graphic artist, fiscal analyst, computer programmer or the architect—positions that require a specific skill and specialized training.

As the outfielder on the baseball team, you have to be able to catch all the fly balls. As the outfielder on your team project, your goal is to minimize all surprises.

You are like an auditor crossing the t's and dotting the i's on the project—making sure there are no loose ends and all procedures are correctly performed.

As you can see, everyone has a role to perform.

Chapter 26

So, Katie, it's been a couple of weeks, have you received any feedback on your job skills?

Katie: No, but my supervisor informed me that I will receive some type of review after six months. Another exam, I thought I was through with taking tests!

Although you have graduated from school, you are not finished with exams. At work, exams come on a different form, called a "performance evaluation."

During the first year, most companies issue some sort of formal evaluation of your work performance. It may be verbal or written, and the initial evaluation usually takes place after the first three months or ninety days of employment.

After the first ninety days, some supervisors evaluate the output of your work, how well you work on the team, and your timeliness.

At the start of your employment, search various websites for various performance appraisal forms. You should familiarize yourself with these forms.

Katie: Why should I review these forms in advance?

When studying for special exams, such as the ACT, LSAT, CPA or GMAT, study guides usually advise you to read the questions first. Whether the exam is in a multiple choice or essay format, reading the questions first, will improve your ability to identify the answers as you are reading.

Using this approach, gives you a heads-up to what the examiner is looking for as you read the problem or essay.

So, when you begin working, you need to know which potential areas your supervisor will test you on. You can obtain a general idea by reviewing basic performance evaluation forms. There is not one specific form and forms may vary per industry or company.

However, most evaluation forms have standard evaluation points including but not limited to:

- **Analytical Ability**: Is the employee able to use her knowledge and technical skills to analyze and solve various problems that occur with the project?
- **Communication**: How well does the employee communicate ideas and responses to inquiries, verbally and written. Does the employee listen well? Does the employee give good presentations?
- **Confidentiality**: Does the employee keep important confidential information to themselves? Or do they share it with unauthorized staff not privy to such information?
- **Dependability**: Is the employee reliable in producing quality work by the requested due dates?
- **Flexibility**: Is the employee approachable? Can they switch gears and work on multiple assignments?
- **Initiative**: Does the employee work independently? Do they take the initiative to solve problems or start assignments on their own?
- **Job Knowledge**: Is the employee able to perform the task and meet the goals of the project?
- **Productivity**: Does the employee produce a sufficient amount of work in a reasonable amount of time?
- **Quality of Work**: Are the employee's projects accurate, neat, user friendly and complete?

- **Team work**: Does the employee get along with his or her coworkers and work amicably on group projects?
- **Time Management**: Does the employee meet project deadlines and come to work on time?

Katie: Wow, they grade you on all of these items? I thought I only needed to get to work on time and complete my assignments.

Chapter 27

Now that you have an idea of how your supervisor will evaluate you, conduct your own self-evaluation.

Be honest with yourself and note your weaknesses. Write them down. Set up a short-term and long-term game plan to improve in the areas you are weak. For example, if you feel your writing skills could use some work, consider taking a business writing class at a community college.

Hopefully, your supervisor will give you interim feedback on your performance. If not, it is okay to occasionally ask for feedback from the boss on how you did on a particular assignment or project. At the end of the day, there should be no surprises on your review.

Katie: *But what if there is a surprise and you feel your supervisor unjustly gave you an overall bad review?*

It does happen. Sometimes the supervisor will get it wrong. In most cases, though, the supervisor got it right, but you could not accept it.

Usually, when the supervisor accurately informs you of your deficits, you already have some inkling of the problems. However, you may not be mature enough to accept that you have these issues.

Let's suppose your supervisor was, indeed, wrong. You have several options.

In your evaluation meeting, ask your supervisor to give you reasons as to why she rated you in this manner. Hopefully her explanation will give you more clarity on the rating.

If you still disagree with the reasons, be prepared to give examples of why she should have given you a higher rating and ask your supervisor to reconsider it. Even though she may agree with you, the supervisor might stick with her own assessment. You can let it go or you can write a response in the employee comments section.

If you decide to write a response related to your disagreement, do not come off angry in the response. Address the issue and give a positive example of your work that warrants a different rating. If possible, let a third party read it to ensure there isn't an angry tone.

Please remember, you are not the first employee to receive an overall negative review. Nor are you the first person to receive a negative rating in a certain category on their performance evaluation.

In most cases, it's simply constructive criticism. You may not understand it at the time of the review, but as time goes on you may reflect on it and understand it better.

Regardless, do not let a bad review hold you back. If anything, over the next couple of months you should prove to yourself and your boss that they got it wrong.

That's what I did. And I magically became the employee of the month three months later. I received the honored parking space and I still have my employee of the month picture.

If you are an A student, on your first evaluation, do not expect to get all A's like you would receive on a report card in grammar school. You may be an above average employee, but you need to grow in some areas.

Yes, there are certain things your supervisor cannot teach you. Let's take, for example, confidentiality. You may already keep pertinent information confidential. Your supervisor does not need to give you an above average grade on this criterion. So don't expect to receive above average marks. It's normal.

If you are an exceptional writer, you may receive an above average grade, not excellent. If this performance appraisal is your first review, there is always room for improvement. Supervisors do not normally give everyone all E's or A's on the first review. If so, where is the incentive for you to grow in the position?

Katie: *You mean to tell me, if I work my butt off in the first year and put in lots of overtime to complete my assignments on time, I will not get all A's?*

No, you might not. Get over yourself. Do not walk around with a chip on your shoulder, giving your supervisor and others attitude. Instead, prove to your bosses you deserve all A's on the next review.

Chapter 28

Speaking of self–improvement:
- It's "ask," not "ax."
- It's "napkin," not "nelpkin."
- It's "you are," not "they is."
- It's "the reason," not "the reason why."
- It's "where are they," not "where they at."
- It's "specific," not "pacific."
- It's "raise the window," not "raise up the window."
- It's "lower the window," not "raise down the window."
- It's "it doesn't," not "it don't."
- It's "supposed," not "posed."

Some employees make these common mistakes, and are not aware of it. It's like having something in your teeth and not knowing. If you make these mistakes, hopefully an acquaintance or colleague will positively point out the errors in your speech or writing. When they do point them out to you, be receptive and thank them.

Communication, as it relates to your writing, pronunciation, speech and grammar, is important in the work place. If you are lacking in these areas do not be embarrassed. You may want to invest in self-improvement classes at your local community colleges. These inexpensive classes usually meet over six to eight weeks, once or twice a week.

Invest in a writing book, such as *The Elements of Style* by William Strunk Jr. and E.B. White, or join an oratorical organization, such as Toastmasters.

If you are a great communicator, share your wisdom. Let your coworkers know they have something in their teeth. Do not look down on your fellow coworkers.

Katie: *Since you mentioned it, there are a couple of things I need to point out to you.*

At work, Katie, at work!

Katie: *Not so fast,* **fellow coworkers** *is redundant.*

Oh, okay. Thank you. As you can see, I'm still a work-in-progress kind of gal.

Katie: *How's that self-editing working out for you? Because you know, you are all over the place.*

Yeah, I know. I like to mix it up.

Chapter 29

So, Katie, did you hear through the grapevine that the secretary is sleeping with her married boss?

Katie: She is?

Well if she is, you need to stay out of it.

Just about every large company has a story like this or a similar one. It's the typical story of a supervisee whose boss began a relationship with another manager in another department.

The boss confided in the supervisee and asked them not to divulge this information to anyone else. Well, you know, as human beings we are social animals. As youngsters and oldies, we must share the juicy details with someone else. The supervisee made the mistake of telling information about the affair to his lunch buddy at work.

Remember rule number one? You have no "best" friends at work when it comes to your personal life? Well, it also applies to the personal lives of your coworkers.

It did not take long for the lunch buddy to run his or her mouth and, eventually, it got back to the boss. Needless to say, life became difficult at work for the supervisee. The supervisee eventually left the company under negative circumstances.

Do not let this tale be your story.

If you have a natural social urge to spread tabloid magazine information about your coworkers—especially your boss—tell it to your girlfriends outside of work.

Not everything is meant for your girlfriends outside of work, either. It's often said there are three degrees of separation. You do not know if a coworker attends the same beauty or nail shop as you. Everyone talks about somebody else's problems in these shops, including your girlfriends.

Likewise, you should never put any gossip in writing or post it on your social network page. And, if you are on social networking websites, such as Facebook or Twitter, I hope you haven't posted pictures of yourself in unflattering or compromising positions.

Katie: *Excuse me?*

Be careful of what you post on these social networks. By now you have seen, heard or read about "A-list" celebrities or other public figures making embarrassing, politically incorrect or potential career ending errors while using these sites. Do not become a "twit-nitwit."

Katie: *I'm just a regular everyday person. Who cares about what I post?*

You never know who is reviewing your postings and may use or hold them against you in the future. Everything you put on these sites is permanent—even after you have closed your page or turned off your account. Items posted previously may have been copied, and people can still find this information.

Your current or future employer can use a search engine to find general information about you. Some of this information could be unfavorable, so why contribute to it by posting this sort of data? Be careful about what you post on these sites.

Chapter 30

So, Katie, do you have control of your personal life as it relates to your finances, mental health and personal relationships?

When you are not happy at home, it will soon show up in your work. Do your research on taking control of your personal life. If your company has an employee assistance program (EAP), utilize it when the need arises. When you use the EAP, it is confidential and it may be an option if you need help regarding personal issues.

Ask the pertinent questions before you go, however, and make sure they do not report to your employer that you sought their help.

If your company does not have an EAP program, search the Internet for mental health message boards or seek referrals from family or acquaintances about counseling. Magazines such as *Women's Day, Essence* and *Good Housekeeping* regularly provide great resources as well.

Regarding your finances, EAP may be able to assist, but the bottom line for most people is to live within your means. It's hard, but it can be done. Be patient, get out of the "I want it now" mode and wait until you can afford it.

Remember our earlier discussion about saving for retirement? Well, you also need a rainy day fund for unexpected events. Catastrophes or misfortunes you do not have any control over will happen and may set you back financially.

Illness, on the job injuries, automobile accidents, house fires and unemployment can set you back financially. Even if you have insurance, it's recommended you have enough savings to cover six months of your monthly obligations in cash reserves.

Since this book is not a self-help book on finance, I suggest you read recommended business books. You can also attend financial planning seminars for guidance. Take control of your finances; do not put yourself in a position where your debts control you. I know, it's easier said than done.

Your boss or your coworkers are not your counselor, finance manager or lawyer. It is okay to ask certain individuals for referrals, but do not bog your colleagues down with your personal problems. Especially your boss, he or she will listen to you in the beginning, but if it becomes a regular issue, it can drain them.

"Certain people get on my nerves and I can't pay my bills."

Although some colleagues try to offer support, they are not your therapists!

Chapter 31

So, Katie, do you multi-task?

Katie: Multi-what?

Most positions require you to be able to juggle multiple projects at once. Everything is needed now. The bosses do not care how many tasks are on your plate, as long as you meet their deadlines.

There are several things you can do to keep the work flowing. First, get organized!

Katie, the tools that I mentioned earlier—did you order them? If so, let's put them into play.

Make yourself a weekly or daily to do list. You can make your weekly list on Friday. This practice will remind you of what you need to complete the following Monday. You can update the list at the end of each day.

Set up a filing system to help you reduce paperwork clutter. You should have an in-basket. Not only should you organize your paperwork, but also organize your electronic files. Set up folders and name them by calendar or fiscal year.

Another important tool to have in your war chest is time management. If you do not manage your time wisely, it could result in a career slowdown.

Your time will not always be **your** time. Depending on where you are on the totem pole, you will either manage the time of others or they will manage your time or both. Does that make sense?

Katie: *No!*

You will need to manage upward, sideways and/or downward.

Katie: *Huh? Now, I am even more confused!*

Okay, you might be a visual learner, so take a look at the pyramid:

Now study the time management table below:

Your Level of Employment: A	Years in Employment: B	Managing Yourself: C	Managing Coworkers: D-Laterally	Managing Supervisees: E-Downwards	Managing Bosses: F-Upwards
Entry:	1-3 yrs	√	√		√
Middle Management:	2-5 yrs	√	√	√	√
Senior Management:	4-7 yrs	√	√	√	√
Chief Executive Officer(CEO):	5-10 yrs	√	√	√	√
Owner:	0-to when you get there	√	√	√	√

Check marks indicate staff you are managing.

Katie: *Wow, that's a lot of people. This chart is kind of busy.*

Okay, I will walk you through this chart. Remember you are on your own at work.

In the first one to three years of your employment (B), you are considered an entry level employee (A). As an entry level employee, your work is frequently dictated by a schedule of due dates. To meet these due dates, you will need to manage:

- Yourself (C)—your own time and work,
- Your coworkers' time and work (D) (laterally), and
- Your supervisor's time and work (F) (upwardly).

Katie: *Why do I have to manage the work of my coworker and supervisor?*

Maybe not directly, but indirectly you will have to occasionally manage their time and work. This is because, generally, most of your assignments are dependent on your colleagues completing their portion of the work.

For example, if you have an assignment that requires your coworker to complete schedule A in order for you to complete schedules B and C, then you need to make sure you get schedule A before you can start. Therefore, you will need to communicate to your coworker that you will be ready to receive his or her work on a specific date.

Katie: *I still do not understand. Why should I have to remind my coworkers to complete their work and forward it to me by a certain time?*

Okay let me put it this way. You are paid bi-monthly on the fifteenth and the thirtieth, correct? If your check is not ready on either of these dates, you do not care that employee A did not forward the time sheets in sufficient time for employee B to process your check. You want your pay check and you want it on time.

You do not care if the supervisor of employee A and B did not sign off on the time sheets—which is the reason employee A was late getting the timesheets to employee B. You want your pay check and you want it on time, period!

Your landlord, your bank and your utility, cable and telephone companies expect their payments by their due dates. End-users of your projects feel the same way and will have the same expectations.

Chapter 32

As you move up the pyramid, you begin to manage everyone's work. Thus, you see check marks in every field of the table.

You need to "CYH" it.

Katie: You mean "CYA"—as in "cover your assets," right?

No, "CYH" it as in "cover your head" when you go outside in the winter. Why catch a cold when you don't have to?

It is called being proactive. Your goal is to make sure you complete your tasks by assigned due dates. You achieve this mission by communicating to your coworkers that you are ready for their part of the work by a certain date.

Managing up or upward, is more about keeping your supervisor apprised of certain key dates or issues related to your projects.

Katie: The CEO or owner—whose time do they upwardly manage?

For either party, it could be: board members, shareholders, customers or employees and regulators from governmental agencies.

Katie: Governmental agencies? They manage the time of government employees?

Have you ever tried to obtain a building permit? Or, tried to get the state to reimburse your agency for work performed six months ago?

Executive employees or owners manage upward the time of others to keep the product or job on task. Phone calls are regularly made to governmental agency heads to prevent a bureaucratic nightmare.

Since you do not make big picture decisions at your entry level position, one would think that you could control much of your own time, right? Wrong!

Unlike school, where you could complete your homework on your own time, you are now part of a team. At work, everyone's assignment is connected to the work of his or her coworkers, all the way to the top of the pyramid and beyond.

When working in a team-oriented environment you are no longer playing singles in tennis, figure skating or boxing. With these sports, when it's time to perform, you are on your own without teammates.

In the workplace, most positions are like positions in baseball, football, soccer and basketball. It takes a group effort to win the game. Each player has to work amicably with their teammates. Although you may be distant and immune from certain behind-the-scene crises, your work is depended on by others and others depend on your work.

Be a team player and learn how to play in a group. Certain positions will allow you to work completely alone. Most positions do not.

Katie: *But I enjoy working by myself. Besides, "Princess Lady Dee" never carries her share of the work. And the person who sits in the next cubicle makes too many mistakes.*

If you plan to move into middle management take advantage of this situation and start indirectly managing your peers. Remind "Princess Lady Dee" of the work she still needs to complete. Correct the mistakes and give guidance to your neighbor.

You are grooming yourself to become a supervisor. You will improve your assertiveness by getting assignments completed on time and dealing with difficult employees.

"Playing with Your Colleagues"

Chapter 33

So, Katie, what are you doing this weekend? Are you hanging out with any of your coworkers?

Katie: But you said I should not have best friends at work. Besides, most of my friends live out of town.

Okay Katie, let me clarify. I came out strongly in the first rule because, as naïve young workers, employees tend to put all their cards on the table when they meet new people. Entry level employees think everyone has their best interest and will do right by them. This is not true.

After a couple months on the job you should gradually be able to figure out who the good guys are. Your bosses or coworkers will invite you to various events outside of work. You will gradually learn how to network.

Katie: Network?

Yes, network. Networking is when you socialize and stay connected with various individuals including:

- current or former coworkers at your company;
- colleagues working at the same company but in different fields;
- colleagues working in the same field but at different companies or industries;
- former college classmates, sorority or fraternity members;

- relatives, friends or acquaintances; or
- other individuals you meet along the way.

Your goal is to share or obtain information that will benefit you in your career or personal life. Back in the day, some people thought networking only happened on the golf course. Now a lot of employees network at many places, like fitness centers, backyard barbecues, after work bars and sporting events.

Katie: I hate going to some of those places. Meeting people you hardly know and making small talk is not fun.

Initially, most of us dislike it. Work on yourself, Katie. It's time to start traveling beyond your normal boundaries and try something new such as vacationing in different states or countries, playing a new sport like tennis or badminton, or taking up a hobby.

Katie: Badminton, really?

You will become more interesting and you will have something to talk about—other than work— when you meet and greet new people.

Make the most of your networking opportunities. You will be surprised what you will learn from your colleagues simply by socializing with them outside of work.

Some work-related advantages might include:

- Getting a jump on new job opportunities before they are advertised or posted after you met the hiring manager at a fundraiser.
- Being selected to work on a special team project after you expressed an interest to the managing partner during a casual conversation at a company picnic.
- Receiving free tickets to a sporting or theater event while bowling with one of the owners of the company.

As time goes by, talking and networking with your peers and colleagues will become easier.

Whatever you do, do not become a chatter box and hog the conversation. Remember to listen and let others get in a word or two.

Just a reminder, you still do not need to put out your personal tabloid information. Save it for your friends outside of work.

Katie: *Well, I started eating lunch with a colleague who works in the graphics department. She's a pleasant person and seems to be trustworthy.*

That's nice. You can maintain the friendship without talking about your drama. You can also wait until either one of you leave the company before you take the friendship to the drama-sharing level. Sharing private information while you are both working at the same company might be asking for trouble.

If you decide to share personal things, make sure the relationship is reciprocal. That is, let your colleague share her information first. If you notice she has not opened up to you with personal disclosures, button up! She must have read this book.

Chapter 34

So, Katie, in the looks department, how would you rate yourself?

Katie: Huh, what kind of question is that?

Believe it or not, how you look does matter in many companies. It's not just whether you are young or old, black or white, skinny or overweight; you might be surprised how people treat you based on your looks, age, culture or economic background.

If you are young, the bookends are going to constantly challenge your intelligence. If you are old, the immature imps are going to think you are senile.

If you are from a certain race or culture, the bigots may apply stereotypes to you. If you are curvaceous or a slim jim, the haters might think you are full of yourself. If you are overweight, they might think you are lazy.

Let's face it; most of us cannot change how we physically look. Regardless of how you look—tall or short, chubby or thin—do not appear sloppy. Pay attention to messy hair, body odor or bad breath. I would suggest keeping a small supply of personal hygiene items such as mouth wash and deodorant in your desk.

If you are a great employee who delivers the product day-in and day-out, sensible bosses will stick with you and not judge you on your physical appearance, culture or economic background.

You cannot change your race or cultural background. You are who you are and some people might have a negative view of your abilities because of who you are. Perform your work, stay professional and hopefully people will judge you on your abilities and not the stereotypes they initially attached to you. Being assertive and having high self-esteem will get you through the judgmental phases.

Some people will project their own insecurities on you. They will give you a hard time in the hope you will eventually give up and go away. You know why? Because they have seen other folks in your position come and go. Because of this they figure that you are no different.

Your goal is to let them know you are here to stay, and you are not backing down regardless of what dodgeballs they throw in your direction.

They might try to rattle you by:
- not giving you adequate information,
- speaking to you in a combative or condescending tone,
- putting you down in front of the boss or other coworkers, or
- challenging you on decisions you make.

Incidents like these are a form of bullying, which happens at the workplace instead of the school yard. In some situations, giving these individuals a taste of honey, instead of vinegar, might work. You don't have to kiss their "assets," but it won't hurt to befriend them by complimenting their work, offering to assist them on a project or shooting the breeze with them about a popular TV show.

Women, more so than men, are much harder on female employees. Although women can be sympathetic and find excuses for bad behavior, they can also be more judgmental and critical of new or younger female coworkers.

"She thinks she's cute; look what she's wearing; I don't like the way she talks to me; who does she think she is, telling me what to do?"

I know I'm going to hear from a few of you folks...okay, a lot of you folks.

Come on now, you know y'all can be catty!

Reminds me of "Insecure Isamella"—number eight on the "Ooogly List"— "I am so afraid that new gal will become the new favorite." Please, do not grow into one of these individuals. If you are already one of them, work on yourself.

Katie: Wait a second, you mean to tell me that men don't have these issues?

They do. Some men do not want you invading their territory either. If a new male is hired on the team, these same catty men don't want the new guy working on the interesting parts of the project. The rude dudes refuse to pass the ball because they do not want the new kid to upstage them.

One more thing, some men in authority act like they are the kings of the paper clips. They will say things like:

"You have to ask me first before you can obtain information from my staff." Or "I will hand over the reports when I am ready to give them to you."

Some men, just like some women - tend to act like unnecessary gatekeepers. They need to work on themselves too!

"Dealing with Reckless Teammates"

Chapter 35

Remember: work is never the problem, it's the people.

"It's them, not you.
It's you, not them.
Well maybe it's both..."

The point is, you can not directly control how people act or respond to you, but you can work on yourself. By improving your actions or reactions, you can indirectly affect the way others respond to you.

Do not let the knuckleheads pull you in. When someone says something controversial to you, do not spar with them. Like they say, "Pick and choose your battles." Just say to yourself or out loud, "umm, hmm, that's nice," and keep walking to your desk or to the restroom.

Back in elementary school, when a classmate hit you and you decided to hit them back, more than likely, you were the one who got caught and reprimanded. Getting caught up in workplace squabbles could be much worse.

When the boss sees you defending yourself or retaliating with words, he may not have seen what initiated your reaction. He will look at you and think, "There she goes again." Or, your coworkers will look at your issues—and you do have them—and blame you for the problem that exists between you and that knucklehead person.

Let these people hang themselves. Eventually, they will. Just take a deep breath, sit back and do not give them a show. If you need to calm down further, say a prayer. It works!

Chapter 36

But there is a difference between knuckleheads and nefarious individuals. Watch out for the nefarious individuals in your midst.

Katie: *Nefarious?*

Yes wicked individuals—"bullies" or "jerks" with issues they will take out on you, if you let them.

Do not become a burden to your supervisor. Do not be the kid everyone picks on, or the kid everyone feels sorry for because he cannot stand up for himself.

Over time you need to learn to stand up for yourself and figure out your own issues. These bullies are no different than the bullies in the school yard. Mom or dad will not always be there to stop them.

There is always a bully at work that you might come up against. Depending on your personality or how you come across to others, bullies usually know which individual they can bother. If you can hold your own with such people, good for you!

For those of you who cannot, you need to stand up to the bully. Bullies will continue to treat you like dirt until you fight back.

Katie: *Physically?*

No, with your words. I repeat: **with your words.** And without the use of foul language.

The bully does not expect you to stand up for yourself. They will continue to push you on the shoulder with their bad attitude until you speak up for yourself. Do not be the person who constantly let these people bother you.

When you need information from the bullies, they usually reply in a harsh manner or do not acknowledge you. But later, when the bully asks you for information, you respond nicely.

When the bully asks for information, continue to respond to them in a professional manner. But the next time they respond negatively toward you, call them on it or have a snappy comeback ready.

Get some courage and practice in the mirror or with a friend. Bullies will not stop until you stop them.

Yes, you can complain to your supervisor, which may make the bully correct him or herself. The change will be temporary though, and the bully will be right back at it the next week.

Katie: *Why is it a burden to my supervisor?*

Your supervisor might feel the need to:

- intervene and obtain the information on your behalf, because you could not obtain the information on your own, or
- defend you because you could not defend yourself.

Your inability to be assertive is now taking time away from the supervisor's other tasks.

Handle your own business. Once you do, it will be refreshing. A lot of your coworkers will openly or silently cheer you on. Then, if the bully tries to go at you again, come right back at them.

For example, if you ask the bully for information and they reply, "I do not know." You can swiftly say, "Okay, I will inform the boss that you stated you do not know." Do not be surprised how quickly they know what you need.

If you do not feel like wasting your time with their attitude, you can always send an email or write a note. Email works best because if the bully does not respond, you have proof. You can send a follow-up email to include their supervisor, if necessary.

Speaking of email, be careful of what you put in writing. Do not respond to or write an email in anger. When you send a negative email, it's permanent. The receiver now has it and can show it to their superior.

Use your business writing skills with emails as you would with business letters or memos. The email represents you—how you communicate. So always proofread your emails and search for misspellings, missing words, incorrect grammar and punctuation.

If you have a long email that gives guidance, ask one of your colleagues to proof read it. Only send emails to coworkers that are work related.

Katie: *If everyone knows the employee is displaying bad behavior toward certain staff, why isn't his or her bad behavior addressed by the supervisor or boss?*

Katie, again, you have to get out of this mindset that life is fair. It's not, especially at work.

Some employees get away with minor offenses, and other employees get away with major offenses, over and over again. For some unexplainable reason, bosses do not address the problem. If they do, they put a Band-Aid on it and the problem returns within a week or a month.

This is another instance that you have to say to yourself, "It is what it is." Handle your business with that person and move on to the next thing.

Chapter 37

Speaking of bullying, let's talk about a dark topic in the workplace: sexual harassment.

You should have learned about this topic in school, but in case you missed the class, sexual harassment is unwelcome sexual behavior that makes an employee feel uncomfortable, uneasy or unsafe.

Sexual harassment comes in various forms including:

- **Verbal:** insulting sexual comments, suggestions, jokes or threats; asking questions of a sexual nature.
- **Non-verbal:** constant staring, writing sexual messages, drawing sexual pictures or making vulgar gestures with body parts.
- **Physical:** violating personal space, unwanted touches, brushing or bumping against someone.

Research the Internet or read pamphlets on sexual harassment for further examples and details.

Sometimes people will test you to see how far they can go. When this happens, you may need to be direct and tell the creep to cut it out.

If you are not sure of the coworker's intentions, or if you think you may have misunderstood him or her, request clarification. A simple, "Excuse me, what did you say?" should suffice. At that point, you put them on notice. If they proceed, take a direct approach and state that you did not appreciate the comment and would like him or her to refrain from this behavior.

If necessary, bring in a third party by stating, "I do not think the human resource department, our coworkers or my lawyer will approve of your comments or behavior."

You do not have to be extreme initially, but you should say something to let the person know that you are prepared to file a formal complaint. This should let the offender know you will not tolerate such behavior. Most of these individuals do not want you telling someone else about them and will refrain from this behavior.

If you are not brave enough to say something, then remember what your mom or grandma told you when you were little: Do not venture alone into places that are dark or creepy.

If you get a bad vibe from a coworker or boss, trust your instinct and never work alone in an office with this individual. If you need to meet with them, make sure the door stays open or someone else is in the room with you.

If it hurts your coworker's feelings, inform them that it is your experience and standard practice to never be alone in a closed space without more than one person in the room. You can leave out the creepy part.

Again, trust your instincts. Until you feel comfortable with this person, do not go into the water.

Chapter 38

All companies should have an official policy regarding sexual harassment. Many women and men who started working in the early 1990's or earlier may feel that they have Anita Hill and other brave women and men to thank for coming forward to share their experience with sexual harassment.

Katie: *Who's Anita Hill?*

Oh yeah, you are still a youngster. This piece of history probably happened before you were born or when you were a toddler.

Anita Hill was an employee who worked for Clarence Thomas at the US Department of Education and Equal Employment Opportunity Commission (EEOC).

In 1991, Ms. Hill testified before the Senate Judiciary Committee, at Mr. Thomas' nomination hearing to become a United States Supreme Court Justice. In that testimony she spoke of incidents that occurred during her employment that could be considered sexual harassment.

Some people may feel that they have Clarence Thomas to thank for making supervisors aware of how their words or behavior can be misinterpreted. They felt he was brave enough to stand his ground and testify that these incidents did not occur. His testimony gave a heads-up to those in supervisory positions to not put themselves in a position to be accused of sexual harassment.

You can research the details of the hearing on the Internet and make your own judgment of which party was telling the truth.

The bottom line though, is that the hearing, at the highest level, put sexual harassment on the front pages of most major newspapers. It was a top story on major news shows. As a result, sexual harassment was no longer pushed under a rug by many companies.

Anita Hill was not the first person to speak publicly about sexual harassment. Ms. Hill's testimony finally gave the urgent attention to the sexual harassment many men and women faced for years. Many companies began issuing formal policies regarding sexual harassment and made it part of their personnel policies.

After the hearings, sexual harassment in the workplace did not stop altogether. But, fortunately for those of us who entered the work force in the early 90's and on, the hearing may have prevented many individuals from having to go through this negative episode during their career.

You do not want to put yourself in a position to be harassed or to be accused of harassing someone else. However, you may not have control over it. Like anything else, sexual harassment can come crashing upon you.

Just because there are laws, or a company has written formal policies in place, does not mean you cannot become a victim or be accused of sexual harassment. If this happens to you, seek legal consultation first, then re-read your personnel policy for guidance. Put the incident in writing with specific locations, dates and times. After you file a formal report with Human Resources, tell your story to another third party besides your lawyer, so they can confirm you mentioned having issues with this individual.

Katie: *What if I do not have funds for a lawyer?*

Contact city, state, federal and/or community agencies such as EEOC, National Organization for Women (NOW), the National Association of Female Executives (NAFE), Gay and Lesbians Alliance

Against Defamation, (GLAAD), Legal Aid or other organizations that assist employees with this issue or point you in the right direction. Their fees may be low and in some cases their consultation or services are free.

Katie: *What if I lose my job?*

Talk to your lawyer or a legal aid organization and let them advise you on the next steps.

Katie: *You are always telling me to research the web or go to some expert.*

Listen, or better yet, read! I'm just telling you what can go on in the work place—giving you some helpful, general guidance on how to handle these various situations when they do occur. I am directing you to resources that could lead you to experts on these specific topics.

Just as your company hired you, the expert—or soon to be expert—to work in a specific position, you too need to seek an expert who can handle particular issues that might occur on the job.

Katie: *Okay, it's your book. You don't have to get so defensive.*

Umm, hmm, that's nice.

Chapter 39

So, Katie, speaking of bad coworkers and you getting on my nerves, are you a weasel?

Katie: A what?

A weasel—it is item number fifteen on the "Ooogly List."

Do not try to score points with your boss by reporting minute infractions about your coworkers to make yourself look good. Things you should not tattle about include:

- he was late again coming to work,
- she made a mistake on the report, or
- they were browsing the Internet.

If anything, your boss is probably aware of such things. The main concern of most bosses is that employees are completing their assignments by the due dates.

Besides, you mean to tell me you never:

- Took an office pen or pencil home—by accident of course…
- Made a telephone call to your friend or relative on company's time…
- Copied or faxed some personal information…
- Returned from a lunch break more than five minutes late…

Katie: No, I have not! You did all of that?

We are not talking about me; I'm just listing a few minor issues. It's still early. You just might break the rules a little.

Do not go running to the boss when you overhear your coworkers saying negative things about someone. You too, will have your day, when the boss gets on your nerves. Stay out of it.

However, there are some items when you will have fiduciary, legal or moral responsibility to report infractions. These items will vary depending on the scope of your position.

Follow your personnel policies, use your common sense, and consult an outside party, such as a lawyer, if necessary. Whatever you do, report it to a third party outside of the job. Someone else other than you can confirm you had concerns about an individual or incident.

Another thing, do not act like a "Related Party Transaction" employee and undermine your boss in front of other employees.

Katie: *Related Party Transaction employee?*

Yeah, another item on the "Ooogly List," it's item number thirteen.

When you have a disagreement with your boss, do not become combative and raise your voice. Other examples of what not to do involving your boss include:

- Do not put supervisors down in front their bosses.
- Do not write an angry response email or memo to your boss.
- Do not use foul language with your boss under any circumstances, even when they are using foul language. You can get your point across without it.
- Do not threaten your boss. Instead, take a deep breath, count to ten, say a prayer and recognize "It is what it is."

Whatever you do, do not lie, cheat, steal or break the law for your boss. It's better to have a dismissal from your job instead of having a felony on your record.

Chapter 40

Katie: *Okay, but what's a Related Party Transaction employee?*

These individuals usually have some kind of connection to the agency. They could be a relative, friend, boyfriend, girlfriend, partner or spouse of the owner or boss. Or they could be a board member's son or daughter or a major customer's relative.

Periodically, they abuse their status or position in the work place. They do so knowing the boss will not fire them. They are complainers who usually do not want to comply with the company's overall mission or the owner's vision. They are reluctant to participate in team building activities.

They will not leave because they probably will not find another company that would put up with them. So they stay and wreak havoc on unsuspecting coworkers who are not familiar with them. Whenever possible, avoid these individuals.

Hopefully these individuals are put in positions where they do not have much contact with other staff. They are not always tucked away in a non-threatening position, however.

If you are unfortunate and have to deal with Related Party Transaction employees on a regular basis, do not let them kill your spirit or your dreams. If you bump heads with them, pick and choose your battles. Sometimes it's not worth the headache. If you do stick up for yourself, the boss already knows they are a pain in the butt.

If anything, do not let them bully you. They usually mess with coworkers who will not stand up for themselves. Let me emphasize, not all employees who have some connection to the company are Related Party Transaction employees. Most connected employees are actually assets to the company and work diligently in the best interest of the company.

Do not underestimate these employees. Connected employees may not have the formal training you have, but they usually know the company's business inside and out. They could probably teach you a thing or two.

Every now and then, you run up against one of these Related Party Transaction employees.

Katie: *Then, why is it tolerated?*

It's another example of item number eleven on the "Ooogly List"— "bosses do not know there is a bad odor in the office."

Katie: *Why is it that everyone sees an issue, but not the boss or senior management?*

Some bosses are clueless there is a problem because it has never been pointed out to them. Other bosses may already know it's there but, for whatever reason, they may not want to do anything about it. It usually takes someone from the outside, such as a new employee or consultant to point this out to the bosses. Only then might the boss realize he needs to address the problem.

In some cases, it's just like telling your friend their significant other is fooling around with someone else. Your friend usually knows it already and doesn't want you to point it out to them. They have excuses for ignoring it and might get mad at you for being the bearer of bad news. In these situations, it is best to stay out of it. Let them figure it out.

Chapter 41

So, Katie, speaking of Related Party Transaction employees, whose daughter or niece are you? How did you get your job?

Katie: I am not a relative. Neither my father nor mother is on the board. I had the right skills and qualifications to obtain the position on my own. Thank you very much!

Now look who's getting defensive!

So a friend or relative did not recommend you. Umm, hmmm. Did you apply through the corporate personnel office?

Katie: Yes.

Umm, hmmm, Anyhow!!....

Regardless of how you got the job, you are representing the person who advised the company to hire you. So you need to prove to the hiring manager that he or she made the right decision by not being a thorn in everyone's side.

It is one thing if the job is over your head. It is another thing if you do not fit in with the team because of your personality.

This person—your friend, relative, employment recruiter or hiring manager—who recommended you for the job, took a chance on you. You need to represent them in a positive manner. Do not embarrass them or make them wish they had never recommended you because of your lack of professionalism.

Do not become item number six on the "Ooogly List"— "The best friend you had no business hiring."

Actions you can control, such as coming to work on time and putting forth your best effort in completing projects, help pave the way for those individuals to advocate for another person to be hired.

The minute you start to become a problem child, you directly or indirectly become a problem for the friend, relative, employment recruiter or hiring manager who recommended you for the position.

Remember that the next time you decide to act out on the job. Always exemplify professional behavior because you are representing others who have a stake in your success.

"Making Moves While Playing on the Inside"

Chapter 42

So, Katie, you have just started your career, what kind of goals do you have?

Katie: *Goals?*

Some of you will already have goals in mind. Others have no clue they should even have a goal or goals, and are just happy to have a pay check.

You are hopping along until one day you notice some of your coworkers are promoted within the company or are moving on to other companies and better positions.

As you begin to meet other staff in other parts of the company, you may start asking yourself or others, "Why do some coworkers have special perks or get to do various things other employees do not?" Such perks include:

· having the summer off,
· coming to work at a later time,
· working from home,
· receiving commissions or bonuses,
· receiving a free destination vacation for good performance, or
· attending parties at the president's home.

Stop worrying about other employees who may have special perks. You need to figure out how you are going to get ahead and get your own perks.

Remember you are a product: you need to invest in yourself. Just like an entertainer, you need to constantly reinvent yourself in order to stay in the game.

Look at the large hamburger chains. In the old days, they would only sell burgers, fries and sodas. Now hamburger chains are selling breakfast, salads, chicken, gourmet coffee—the works.

To stay in the game, you need to expand your skills so you have more to offer your current employer, a future company or a company owned by you.

You can improve your abilities in several ways: obtain a higher degree, such as a master's degree; obtain various job related certifications; obtain another degree or specialized training in a different field.

If you are going to work all your life and not start a business, you may need to acquire additional education mastering areas in which you plan to work.

You might start out thinking, "I am just going to be here a couple of years." But, when you look up five years later, you might still be working in the same place you began with no improvement of your professional development.

You gained some experience, but did you grow, and if so, how much?

Chapter 43

Katie: But I already have a huge outstanding student loan balance, and the company will not pay for my tuition. Besides, I am tired of school.

Let's address each one of your excuses—backward!

First, you do not have to go back to school right away. It's okay to take a break. While you are on that break, if you are single and do not have children at home or do not need to take care of a relative, get a part-time job. Just because the company won't pay for it does not mean you cannot invest in yourself.

You do not have to go back to school full-time, either. Most loans allow you to enroll in a thirty-year repayment plan, thus allowing you to have a low monthly payment. Of course, you will pay more interest, but it might be worth the investment. Check to see if there are scholarships, loan deferrals or forgiveness programs.

You probably have other mountains as to why you cannot go to school.

Katie: If you mean reasons, then yes, I do have other reasons!

No, I meant excuses! Do not let an excuse be your mountain as to why you cannot accomplish something. All through life, mountains will be placed in front of you. When that mountain gets in your way, figure out a way to drill right through it or get around it.

While you are at it, read *Rich Dad, Poor Dad* by Robert T. Kiyosaki. If working for someone else is not your cup of tea, Mr. Kiyosaki has a few ideas on how to get your own.

Until then, this job is your career. Yes, you may change directions in your career, but if you have been doing the same exact thing for the last five years, you might as well work in a factory on an assembly line.

Is this the kind of job you signed up for?

Katie: What's wrong with working in a factory? My dad worked forty-three years in the automobile factory. He fed a family of six, put three of his four children through college, owns his house, and is now living comfortably on his monthly pension!

Whoa, Katie, slow down. No one is trying to talk bad about your dad or your mom. Yes, one can make a decent living working on assembly lines in certain industries. But is this the reason your parents paid for your college education? For you to work in the same position for over thirty years?

Anyhow!!..., let's get back to my point.

Educating yourself can come in a number of different forms. If your employer offers some form of tuition reimbursement, take advantage of it. Since you may work at the company for several years or more, you might as well let the company pay for your schooling. But note that most companies will require employees to stay a couple of years after graduation.

Once you obtain additional degrees and certifications, do not wear it on your arm like a tattoo. It's nice you have your MBA, CPA or doctorate and you should be proud of it, but don't shove it down your coworkers' throats.

Otherwise, when your colleagues see you coming down the hall, they might think, "Here comes the Most Bankable Airhead, the Certified Parking Attendant or Doctor Dufus."

Also, when other employees obtain their certifications or doctorates, don't you speak ill of them. If your coworkers request you call them doctor and put letters behind their name, respect their decision.

Expanding your education is not just limited to going to graduate school, however. You can grow as an individual by taking fun classes, such as acting, cooking, dancing or drawing.

Taking such classes can increase your networking base. You may meet other professionals like yourself, working for other large companies. You may even meet your future significant other—Mr. or Mrs. Right.

The point is, you need to do something. Set some obtainable goals for yourself.

Chapter 44

So, Katie, how's the networking going for you? Have you met any new colleagues outside of your department or company?

Katie: I met a couple of new employees who also started around the same time I did.

Oh, so you probably stumbled across the hidden job market.

Katie: What's the hidden job market?

On any job, whether the company is small, medium or large, you will come across the hidden job market.

The hidden job market consists of unique or ideal jobs that you did not know existed. They are not usually posted in the newspaper ads or ordinary places that you would search for a job. These positions may be available only at a certain company or in a certain industry. Employees stumble across these positions when they go to work at their companies.

New employees meet individuals who are working in the positions or they see the positions posted on the employee boards. Other employees may read about the positions in a newspaper or magazine article.

Instead of advertising, some companies use employee search firms to locate individuals for these particular positions. Other companies create the jobs based on a need and hire from within the organization.

Katie: Can you give me examples of these kinds of jobs?

It could be anything, including:
strategic operations planner, instructional coach, grant writer, communications director, window display coordinator, costume jewelry regional sales manager, transportation manager, publicist or public relations manager, Christmas tree decorator, graphic artist, anesthesiologist, liquor salesman, best boy, giftware buyer, audience prep manager, overseas travel coordinator, special events coordinator, insurance form editor, import/export expeditor, human resource benefits coordinator, medical transcripts coordinator, food broker, athletics department equipment manager, construction engineer, insurance underwriter, actuary, radio show producer, stylist, data analyst, delegate operations manager, merchandiser manager, set decorator, voice over actor, clip art artist, etc.

Katie: *Okay, I'm puzzled. I've heard of some of these positions. What's hidden about them?*

The positions are hidden only if you were not aware of them.

As you come across some of these occupations, one of them may grab your interest. As you reinvent yourself, you may want to seek out the training required to obtain these kinds of positions.

Katie: *I am just getting started in my new career and I do not see myself doing anything else right now.*

Maybe not today, but after a year or two you might stumble across an ideal position. When you get to know other individuals that have worked ten to fifteen years—either within your company or at other companies—you will see they did not start in the same kind of position they are working in today.

Katie: *You mean to tell me that I could be working at this company for the next ten years?*

When I was your age, and just entering the workforce, I said the same thing too. Whatever you do, do not count on the lottery—count on yourself to take you to the next level.

Everyone has more than one talent. Look at your favorite entertainer. Nine times out of ten he or she can sing, dance, and act. Many actors go behind the camera and direct movies or become the executive producer of films or television shows.

Some of your favorite singers may have been back-up dancers for other major stars. He or she might have installed gas meters or sold automobiles in their former life. If you have spoken to any of your professors, they will tell you they worked in various fields before deciding to teach. Some people turn their hobbies into a business or realize that they can get paid by a company working on that hobby.

Many people study in a particular field or choose a career they consider safe to find a job. They realize later there is something else they really want to do. Most employees have this revelation when they come across other individuals working in ideal jobs the employee did not know existed—jobs in the hidden job market.

Chapter 45

Which leads me to the next question:

So, Katie, you have been working several months. When was the last time you updated your resume?

Katie: I have not thought about it, why?

Well, you know that initial resume you provided the company to obtain interviews for this job? It will be obsolete in another six months.

Although it has been only a couple of months, believe it or not, you have acquired some new skills.

Katie: I have?

Yes, you have! After the six month threshold, you should consider revisiting your resume. It may not seem like a lot, but you have additional skills you can add to your resume.

Katie: Such as?

Depending on your job, it could be a variety of things. Here are some potential items:

- training workshops or seminars you attended or presented at;
- reports, flow charts, schedules or forms you created or updated;
- budgets you oversaw, monitored or created;
- membership in professional organizations or company sub-committees;

- projects you completed—including video presentations, program manuals, operating procedures;
- office equipment or software programs you used to complete your work;
- supervisory roles on various projects; or,
- annual audit or monitoring visits in which you participated in or assisted your boss preparing for.

As you can see, your resume is steadily growing each time you take on a new assignment and assist your boss or coworkers with projects.

"Switching Positions"

Chapter 46

So, Katie, there is another reason you should always keep your resume updated.

Katie: What's that?

Airplanes, automobiles, boats and trains.

Katie: Huh?

Transition time! Just like transportation, transitioning out of your job and moving on to another department, company or venture can occur in various forms. It is usually initiated in one of two ways.

By your decision:

- You applied for a new position in another division or company.
- You took a leave of absence from work due to illness or other personal matters.
- You returned to school full-time.
- You decided to work part-time.
- You started your own business.

Or, by your employer's decision:

- They promoted you to a higher position.
- They transferred you laterally to another division.
- They laid you off due to the company's poor performance.

- They fired, demoted or transitioned you out of the company for poor performance.

Since examples of your decision to transition and the first three examples of the employer's decision are pretty straight forward, let's tackle the last one on the employer's decision list.

Sometimes you can see a firing, demotion or transition out of the company coming and although you tried, you cannot fix it. Other times it comes as a surprise—like a car crash—and hits you out of nowhere.

Getting fired or demoted can cause you to doubt yourself. Up to this point, you succeeded in just about everything in which you applied yourself: you won the science fair, was crowned homecoming queen, made the dean's list and you were voted president of your sorority chapter. But for some reason, you could not make this particular milestone in your life a success.

There could be a variety of reasons why it occurred—the dodgeballs:

- You did not possess the skills necessary to complete your assignments.
- You dropped the ball on a major project, thus costing the company money and/or a major client.
- Although you had the skills, your horrific attitude did not allow you to give good customer service.
- You got caught up in office gossip and it spun out of control.
- You had poor attendance.

Most likely, not one of these issues by itself was the reason for your downfall. It probably started off as one or two small snowballs and it slid downhill like an avalanche.

Somewhere along the way you lost control, or you never had control from the beginning.

Maybe personal issues affected your work and led to you being fired or demoted. Some examples include:

Physical or mental illness, relationship problems, financial problems, taking care of a family member, addiction or childcare issues.

These issues could have led to poor time management, lack of focus and an inability to work amicably with the team.

If none of these items were an issue, then maybe your boss or coworkers were not ready for your amazing talent or grand personality.

Katie: *What do you mean?*

Sometimes when people hire you, they tell you they want you to do all of these wonderful things in the position. When you start working in the position, actually performing the work they described, your employers realize they are not comfortable with your approach to the work.

Although they wanted change, they were not ready for your version of change. It may not have dawned on you to take baby steps instead of gigantic steps. Along the way, you and the boss stop seeing eye-to-eye.

Furthermore, you were not clicking with your new coworkers. You simply could not figure out the peculiar culture of the company's work environment.

It does not matter who was at fault, either you or your employer. Know that you will recover from this temporary setback.

The point is, it's important you understand the reason the firing happened. This way, you can better equip yourself to handle or avoid similar situations that may arise at a future job.

Chalk it up to a learning experience. You are not the only employee who has gone through this specific episode in their career.

Katie: *Were you fired? Never mind, I won't ask.*

Then, don't!

Do not let this story define who you are as a person and your capability to perform in this particular line of work.

While you are on the job, it is important to network with your peers or consultants. These coworkers and external contacts are individuals who can attest to your work and hopefully you can use them as references for future employers.

Chapter 47

Before you say or repeat something, think:

Is it true? Is it kind? Is it necessary?

A coworker gave me this quote. I am not sure where it originated but the quote speaks volumes to me. So much so, that I have it posted on my filing cabinet.

Make a part of your ongoing professional development to read or post items that are positive and encouraging.

So, Katie, speaking of being kind, are you one of those people who have difficulty apologizing?

Katie: *I don't think so.*

Recognize when you are wrong. It's okay to say, "I'm sorry." There are several ways to say, "I'm sorry" without having to speak the words aloud.

If you are one who has a hard time owning up to your own issues, it will be hard for people to respect you.

As imperfect human beings, at many points in our lives we will put ourselves in the "I'm sorry" position. We will make mistakes, we will hurt someone's feelings and we will not only make this gaffe in our personal lives but also in the workplace. It happens!

Yes, Katie, it will happen to you.

The goal here is to reduce how often you hurt someone's feelings. This usually comes with maturity.

If you are great at something, do not belittle someone who is not as great an achiever as you are. Instead, assist them. Believe it or not, assisting your coworker will prepare you for a promotion and help you grow as a leader.

By assisting your colleagues, you are gaining experience in giving directions, overseeing or reviewing the work of others and allowing others to view you as a role model. You are becoming a person who can lead a team and get an assignment completed.

If you are good at what you do, you do not have to brag about it. Your work speaks for itself. Learn how to be a good coworker. Remember, everyone in the organization provides customer service to someone besides the public.

The company hired you to provide a service. Your customers may not be exactly people purchasing the end product. Instead, your customer may be your coworker who works at the next desk, a different department or another location.

The receptionist or administrative assistant who answers the phone is usually the first point of contact with the company. But your position could be the first point of contact as well.

Hopefully, your company hired staff with people skills. Someone who is friendly, pleasant and competently represents the company with good bedside manners. Unfortunately, this ideal situation is not always the case. There are employees that have nasty dispositions and awful attitudes.

You will meet these people too! They know how to turn on the nicey-nice for the boss. They do not mess with certain important individuals because they know the repercussions if they did. These intentional actions let you know that these individuals are manipulative and not stupid (though they probably have a screw loose somewhere). Still, don't let these dreadful employees take you off your game.

You need to stay consistently on your game. Yes, you are going to have some terrible days when you will not want to be bothered, but you need to check that bad attitude or what happened to you before you arrived that morning at the door. If you realize that you are "that person," work on yourself and if necessary, get some help or therapy.

Chapter 48

So, Katie, are you an A, B or C player?

Katie: There you go again with these weird sayings.

Umm, hmm, that's nice.

Well, I am not referring to that old anecdote where the "A" students go on to teach as professors at the universities, the "C" students go on to own businesses and the "B" students go to work for the "C" students.

"B" players are usually perfectionists. If you are one, do not be so hard on yourself when you make a mistake and do not get defensive when someone points out your mistake.

"C" players are usually careless with their work. Their supervisor has to keep returning the work back to them to fix obvious mistakes.

But an "A" player is competitive. They play to win and they are your go-to person.

Katie: The go-to person?

Yeah, be the go-to person, not the "do I really have to go to her person."

Make yourself indispensible by being the left and right hand of your boss. When it comes to layoffs, you will not be the first person on the list of people your boss could do without and cut from the employment rolls.

The **go-to person** gives you the big reveal when the project is complete. They give you more than you can imagine, just like the designers on home decorating TV shows.

- The "do I really have to go to her" person gives you the blah and the boss has to send the project back to the drawing board.

The **go-to person** will make a delicious broccoli salad that is out of this world and puts all the finishing touches on the project.

- The "do I really have to go to her" person will leave out important ingredients and leave the project incomplete.

The **go-to person** is like your best caterer—they deliver your food on time and meet deadlines on a regular basis.

- The "do I really have to go to her" person always has an excuse as to why the food is cold and could not meet the boss's request to serve it by the 6:00 p.m. deadline.

Katie: *Okay, okay, I get it. You have been watching a lot of those cooking and home makeover shows again, right?*

Well, it certainly helps in the creativity department and I do enjoy watching HGTV.

Chapter 49

Get into the "Hey Now" mode. Compliment your coworkers and try to maintain a sunny disposition, when you walk into the work place. Smile and greet everyone.

Katie: *But she never speaks to me.*

Who?

Katie: *The gal who works in the communications department. Whenever I pass her in the hall and say hello, she turns her head and keeps walking.*

Then don't speak to her! And she has the nerve to work in communications? Reminds me of "Mz. America," number four on the "Ooogly List"— "It's all about me."

You are going to have some knuckleheads in your midst. Speak to them on the first day and again on the second day. If they still do not respond, leave them alone. Do not give them the time of the day. Eventually, if you continue to rise in the company, these knuckleheads will come looking for you and try to befriend you on Facebook.

Even if you do not rise up the ladder anytime soon, some of these knuckleheads will start wondering why you no longer greet them. So, they may test you and try to speak to you first.

It's okay to return the greeting, but the next time you see them, don't you dare speak to them first! Let the knuckleheads continue to speak to you first. He or she already had a chance for you to take the initiative and be polite to them.

Over time, if you believe the knucklehead has become civil and a normal human being, it's okay to greet them again. But you know what they say: "Once a snake, always a snake." Let them in your inner circle, they will bite you.

Chapter 50

So, Katie, you are not one of those needy individuals, are you?
Katie: What do you mean?
The kind of person who is always looking for a thank you, or an acknowledgement for a completed project. Be aware, you will not always get it. Do not become needy.

You may have worked long hours on a project and when it is finally completed the boss may publicly acknowledge you. Or they may acknowledge someone other than you. Some bosses may even take the credit for the whole project themselves.

When it first happens to you, drink a lot of water to swallow this marshmallow. Over time, you will see, it's the norm in many places. Again, you do not control things, yet.

Right now, your position is like a cameraman working on a movie set. You need to understand that you are not the star of this project. Your company hired you as part of the behind the scenes movie crew to make a great Oscar award-winning movie.

At awards time, only the stars and director will receive the accolades. If you are not one of them, get over it. Your time will come but you will have to make your own niche, just as your boss and your coworkers have done.

Later, when you are in the boss's position, try to remember to acknowledge, if not publicly then privately, the folks who assisted you on various projects.

So, Katie, if you are not needy, do you like being the center of attention?

Katie: Why do you ask? Do you have another "Do Not?"

As a matter of fact, I do. If you are a drama queen or king, try to minimize it at work.

Another "Do Not" is, do not try to obtain headlines before your time.

Katie: What headlines?

Like any owners or coaches of a sports team, some bosses have huge egos. It's their show and you are just one of a few talented individuals chosen to play on the team.

Your job is to make money for the owners. You make them money by winning games each week. Some of the players will show some personality, which builds up a fan base and helps increase the advertising revenues. Some owners or coaches do not want you to upstage them, however. Remember, it is not about you. If it was, you would have your own team or company.

You do not move up the ladder by making the bosses look bad. You are replaceable. In the current market, there are at least ten potential employees waiting to take your spot.

As you gain more experience, your skills will become more in demand. Let your work speak for itself and others will do the bragging for you.

Chapter 51

So, Katie, you are taking the lead on a brand new project?

Katie: Yes. My boss chose me to update the company's product manual. Other department heads will use the manual as part of their sales presentation to new clients.

Good for you! But you need to be aware of the sideline cheerleaders.

Katie: Sideline cheerleaders?

Yeah, that's what I call them. They are number one on the "Ooogly List." You have seen these "Ms. Know-it-all" folks before in various forms.

Sideline cheerleaders act like film critics, but in a negative way. They always want to criticize what you do, but never have the courage or want to invest the time to make a movie.

Sideline cheerleaders are the ones who criticize the dance moves you chose when the gym teacher chooses you to be the pom-pom team captain. These same students never offer any suggestions of their own, just complaints.

Sideline cheerleaders are coworkers who act like pain-in-your-butt baseball parents. They always want to criticize the decisions volunteer coaches make regarding their son or daughter's baseball teams. These same parents never want to step up and coach a team themselves, though.

Do not let these sideline cheerleaders get in your way or make you doubt yourself as a project leader. You will make some mistakes and stumble from time to time. But do as grandma says, and "Just pick yourself up and dust yourself off. Go right back at it."

Nevertheless, not every criticism is without merit. Your boss or coworker will provide constructive criticism you need to consider.

Katie: *Constructive criticism? How is any criticism nice?*

It's feedback that is positive and beneficial to your project. The useful information could include items you did not consider. Or it could include changing a key aspect of the project that you may want to keep.

Try to remain open to such suggestions and ideas. You may not need to include all of his or her ideas but some of the suggestions will probably improve your project.

Chapter 52

So, Katie, how are you going to start the project?

As with anything, before you turn in a completed project or report, remember to dot your I's and cross your T's. As they say, "Perform your due diligence."

Katie: *Due diligence?*

Yes, approach the work with great care and thoroughness.

One of the first things you will learn on the job is solutions are in the details. Pay attention to the details of your assignments.

Try to figure out in advance the questions the boss or end users will ask you. Then, answer the questions before you give the project to your boss.

Also, take an overview of your project:

- Is it user-friendly?
- Is it logical?
- Does the document have great visuals, or is it easy on the viewer's eyes?
- Did you test it on some of your coworkers?
- Did you have someone proofread it or search for proper punctuation, misspellings or missing words?
- Did you "smooch it?"

Katie: *Do you mean KISS it? As in 'Keep It Simple Stupid'?*

Yeah, that too, but I was referring to "Show me only the crap I need."

Katie: *Huh? S.M.O.T.C.I.N.? Aren't you off on a couple of words?*

Katie, it is not meant to be an acronym.

After a few projects, you will soon figure out your boss's management style and needs. Some bosses just want the bottom line and do not want too much unnecessary data or paperwork. Other bosses do want supporting documentation along with the bottom line.

Sometimes it depends on the type of project; bosses preferences vary between having a lot of data or just the bottom line. Experience working with your boss will help you understand his or her wants and needs.

"Exiting the Game"

.

Chapter 53

So, Katie, how did you do on the project?

Katie: It was challenging, but I think I did okay. Thank you for the tips. Hopefully, my boss will give me more interesting projects.

Great, this project is an additional item you can add to your resume.

Katie: By the way, when should I ask for a promotion and a raise?

Well, Katie, you just started working in the position. It may be a while before someone recommends you for a promotion. Then again, an opportunity may present itself. It could come quickly due to a vacancy or a newly created position.

There is no magical formula. Each company is different on how it awards raises and promotions. In some companies, you may be put on a one-to-three year career track. If you successfully complete a training program, you are automatically promoted to the next level with an increased salary. In other companies, you may have to apply for open positions in order to get promoted and an increased salary.

Katie: Suppose there are no open positions?

Well you can do what I did, ask for one. Before you ask for one, though, there are a couple of things that you need to consider or have in place.

Katie: Such as?

Like I stated earlier, you just got started. Over the next year, you need to continue to build on your resume. Take on additional projects—do not wait to be asked. Volunteer when you see a need in your department, be proactive and take on the task.

Consider all of the suggestions mentioned earlier and throughout this book. Work toward being the go-to person as well as being your supervisor's right and left hand. Your goal is to have a great performance review under your belt.

Katie: *How does one ask for a raise?*

You can mention it verbally to your supervisor, but I advise you to put your request for a raise or promotion in writing. You do not want to receive a knee-jerk no to a verbal request.

By putting your request in writing, it gives your supervisor or senior management time to review your accomplishments and thoughtfully consider your request.

Start by writing down a list of your accomplishments. What's on that list is going to let you know when it is time to ask. If the list, in your mind, is pretty impressive, you will know.

Share your list with someone outside the company, such as a mentor, colleague and/or career counselor. They will give you constructive feedback on your list. Put the list in a business letter format and give it to your boss or immediate supervisor. You can purchase a business letter writing book or search the Internet for examples of these types of letters.

Remember, this letter should be in your voice. You are only reviewing examples of the request letter to get an idea of how to write one.

Again, make sure someone outside your company reads the letter before you share it with your supervisor. Hopefully, you have a supervisor who will recognize your extraordinary talents and go to bat for you.

Chapter 54

Katie: *What if they say, No?*

They just might say no. As with anything, you won't know until you ask.

If you get a no, do not consider it a rejection or a failure on your part. Hopefully they will give you reasons for the no. If not, ask for an explanation.

There could be several reasons for the rejection. Some reasons are valid while other reasons are lame excuses. Whatever the reason, process it and think it through carefully. If necessary, seek advice from a colleague or mentor.

Great employers recognize that in order to retain or attract great employees, the company needs to provide a path for growth for existing employees. Continue to gain knowledge and skills while working in your current position. This proactive step is going to keep you in the control position.

Be patient. Just because the bosses said no at this time does not mean they will not consider you for a promotion at a later time, perhaps in the near future.

Also, you do not want to develop a pattern of job hopping on your resume.

Katie: *What's job hopping?*

It's when you worked two years or less at three different companies for your last three positions. With a record of job hopping, potential employers might consider you a risk and take a pass on hiring you. If they feel you will not stay with them for an extended period of time, new employers do not want to invest their time and money to develop you.

However, as you continue to work, you might begin to realize the only way for you to get promoted is for someone to retire or leave. Or, you may realize that getting a promotion to a higher position is political—you have to know someone in order to move up a notch or two.

Although, you need to be patient with your progress, you do not need to wait forever to get what you desire. They did not give you your degree; you earned it on your own. Once you feel you are ready to move on, make the move.

Like everything else, it's a gamble. You have already taken chances on yourself. Going to college put you in a place to obtain a higher paying position.

Hang on to your current position while you look for a new one, though. Depending on the economy, it may take some time to find new work.

Dedicate the same amount of time and attention as you did with your current position to seek out your next ideal job. Hopefully, the networking advice will pay off for you.

Chapter 55

So, Katie, there are other avenues in which employees receive increases in pay.

Katie: *Such as?*

Depending on the company and the job, you may be part of a union. If so, your union may have negotiated a contract with your company so your position receives an automatic pay increase each year.

Also, since you are a professional employee you may be an "exempt" employee.

Katie: *Yes, I found out about that the hard way.*

A few weeks ago, I was working a lot of overtime hours and the supervisor informed me and some other entry level coworkers that "exempt" positions do not receive overtime pay.

Yes, most positions are categorized as either exempt or non-exempt. In exempt positions, you work until the assignment is complete. Therefore, you may work beyond the normal eight-hour shift on some days and your regular paycheck is not increased.

However, if you work an excessive amount of overtime, smart bosses usually give exempt employees comp time. That is, time you can take off from work without having to use personal time or vacation days.

By law, employers must pay employees in non-exempt positions overtime pay. Companies pay these employees time-and-a-half after the number of hours worked exceeds a certain number of hours per day or week. It's usually eight hours per day or forty hours per week.

However, labor laws may vary by state. You can check your state's website for various regulations that apply to your state.

Also, if the economy is doing well and the company is profitable, most companies give all employees a COLA or merit raise.

Katie: *COLA?*

Yes, and I am not referring to Pepsi or Coke.

Cost of living allowance or COLA are salary increases based on an annual index and increases usually range from one to five percent of the employee's base salary. Merit increases are based on the employee's job performance. These increases are usually five percent or more of the employee's base salary.

If you know the job market is tight, you might want to consider staying put at your current company. But, if you are not happy and do not feel you are growing—and can no longer maintain your sanity—make the move.

As they say, you might have to take two steps backward before you can make a great leap forward.

"Epilogue"

Chapter 56

So, Katie, you might be thinking, "Why should I take your advice or recommend this book to someone else?"

I was in your place many years ago about to take this journey. So many of us are clueless to what lies ahead for us.

I am laying out a road map that will not solve all of your problems. I hope the map will guide you in making some smart decisions when you are confronting different issues that may arise in the work place.

Although I researched information to verify some of the material presented, I am not a professional researcher. What I do have is over twenty-five years of experience working in various companies small, medium and large.

I have worked in male and female dominated workplaces, union based jobs, start-up companies and family-owned businesses.

Over the years, I interviewed, supervised and actively mentored interns and entry level employees, both young men and women alike.

There is a difference between someone you want to emulate and someone who actively takes you under his or her wings. You can learn something from both individuals.

People who you want to emulate may not be accessible, but you can take notes on what they do from afar.

If you are fortunate to come across someone who is willing to take you under their wings, do not dismiss their sometimes over-the-top advice. It will eventually come in handy.

As undergrad students, we may have taken a lot of business related courses focusing on the business, legal and psychological aspects of the work place. You learned a great deal of terms and theories about successful people and organizations. You wrote papers and prepared projects.

For the most part, after the course was completed, you were happy to be done with that class. Even when you had to work on group projects or attend classes, you pretty much dealt with classmates for no more than three to six hours per week. So, if someone in the group made it difficult to complete the project, it was only for a semester.

As a student, you did not grasp that you are going to start working with some difficult people for at least eight to ten hours per day, five days a week, fifty-two weeks a year, for several years. That is a lot of time for someone to get on your nerves.

Some of your coworkers will become life-long friends, even after you have left the company. But all of the employees will become part of your foundation and a piece of the building block of who you will become in the work force.

Chapter 57

So, Katie, I think I have given you enough information to keep you going and make it through your first year of employment.

Sooo, Katie, I ask you again, in another way—

ARE YOU READY TO PLAY DODGEBALL?

Okay, are you now prepared to go to work?

Katie(s): *Of course!*

Then, let's go to work!

Remember, in the work environment, the bosses are not always going to do things that are fair, that make sense or are done your way!

It's their kingdom, and until you're the boss with your own company, you have to play by **their** rules. Once you get your own, you still gotta play by **their** rules.

If you don't believe me, ask a media mogul, a real estate tycoon or the president.

Hey, you hung out with me and made it to the end!

Leave a comment on my Facebook page and let me know your thoughts on the book:

www.facebook.com/avoidingthedodgeballs

Feel free to post a review of the book on various book review websites, such as:

- www.amazon.com
- www.barnesandnoble.com
- www.goodreads.com

Not signed up on Facebook?

Then send me an email at:

e.marie@notadisgruntleemployee.com

Thank you for reading!

<<<<<<<<<<<<<<Teaser Alert>>>>>>>>>>>>>>

Hey Katie, look at you! All dolled up with your power suit, new hair style and Chanel purse. Life must be treating you grand!

Katie: Hello. How are you? It's good to see you again. By the way, you can call me, "Kate".

My, my, aren't we sophisticated now? Well, you will always be Katie to me. However, I will respect your wishes and call you Kate.

So Kate, it's been almost two years. What's been going on? How's the job coming along?

Kate: Great! I recently received a promotion and I am the new manager of the Buying Department. I have five employees reporting to me.

We really need to get together. I have so much to tell you. Here's my business card.

Oh, you have business cards. Well I have to check my schedule and I might can do lunch with you sometime next month.

Kate: Next month? I really need to talk to you sooner. Can we meet after work? Like today? Please!

Okay, okay. Let me see if I can move some appointments around on my schedule for this evening or this weekend. I'll give you a call later this afternoon, or better yet, why don't you purchase my next book in the series…

Avoiding the
Dodgeballs

. . .At Work 2.0

"Katie gets promoted to Middle Management"

Acknowledgments

I would like to thank the Lord, my husband, daughter and grandson, as well as family, friends, acquaintances, colleagues, authors, consultants, professionals, public radio and strangers who gave me the inspiration and encouragement to write *Avoiding the Dodgeballs....At Work.*

Special thanks go out to a young lady, Ms. Geneva—who unknowingly pushed a button inside to remind me I am still young and I have a few more goals to complete. It was Geneva's own goals and dreams about herself and her college classmates she shared with me that got me started on writing this book.

Listen to and support public radio. A public radio interview with a recently successful self-published author lifted me over my first hurdle in writing this book. When I thought my initial sixteen-page stab at writing was only a term paper or magazine article, Amanda's interview persuaded me to make a another attempt at writing.

She discussed her ups and downs in writing her books and finally getting her work published. The best advice I drew from the interview was to treat my writing as if it was a job.

The grace of God continued to place people, book events, magazine articles and other related items in front of me that encouraged me to keep writing this book until it was completed. Along the way, I attended Erika Gilchrist's seminar and purchased her book *How to Write and Publish Your Book, Now!* I would like to thank Erika and other great authors, such as my friend and colleague Jean Jennings—*Hidden Hurts Revealed*; O. Keeys (Omegia)—*Not So Common Sense Guide for Authors*;

John Desjarlais—*Bleeder*; Henry Abraham— *How to Write a Book in 90 Days God's Way;* Delois Dorsey (Auntie), Paula Foster, Bertha Buchanan and Dr. Leonard Ingram, all who shared with me their experiences and insights on writing, publishing and marketing books.

Thank you to the various interns and supervisees who I mentored over the years, and various colleagues, supervisors and bosses who mentored me along the way. You directly and indirectly provided me with a foundation for the writing of this book.

Thank you, for your kind words of encouragement on this project: Brenda Dobbins-Noel, Portia Kennel and Cynthia Crim (former supervisors and mentors), Sherita Dorsey (sister-in-law), Rachael Harris (my BFF), Audrey Long (cousin), Alicia Meyer (cousin), Em"ma" Robinson and Michelle Clark (Mickey, my SFF—sis/friend forever) and Gail Thomas (St. Bernadette soccer mom and friend).

Rachael, your gift of pajama's kept me warm while I was editing the book. Alicia, you recommended a great videographer Robert Gorman - Sonrise Video Productions. Bob, you did a great job shooting the video and assisting me in developing the story behind the book.

To my coworker, Donnie Roberson (IT support) – although you did not know why I asked the questions, thank you for giving me helpful hints on how to download various software products and how to use them.

Thank you, Dr. Myra Sampson and Gladys Simpson, (supervisors and mentors), – Dr. Sampson on one occasion, you read about a dozen of emails issued by me. You unknowingly gave me a chuckle and some form of validation when you said to me, "Emerah, you must like to write."

Thank you to the account coordinator, Katherine Davis and to the editing, cover design and interior layout teams at CreateSpace.com.

Thank you to the "Take Another Look" – reviewers and editors: Angela Baquet, Kenyatta Dorsey, Kenneth Jones and Laura Kenton

Thank you to the "Take One More Look before We Go to Print" - reviewers and editors: Wilma Burns and Theresa Connolly

Thank you to the "Cover Design" selection committee:

- **Team Blue:** Sherri Clark and Steve Freeman
- **Team Yellow:** Stephen Betts, Patrice Dorsey, Jean Jennings, Michelen Miller and Julius O'Leary

Thank you, for your services and coming to my rescue:

- Graphic artist, ad and website designer: Valeda Williams
- Graphic artist: Alex Dorsey (nephew)
- Printer: Arvind Bhargava (Microprint)

You guys and gals rock! I am grateful for your invaluable input on this project. I hope everyone is available for my next book.

Mom, thank you for that much needed kiss on the forehead, and those words of wisdom: "No one will take care of your child as well as you would." Thank you for making sure God was a huge part of your chidren's upbringing, and your wonderful cooking, which included those delicious deserts—batter-licking homemade cakes, cookies and chocolate fudge.

"Deddy," thank you for coming home every night, taking us kids to your Sunday softball games, introducing us to a world of possibilities, taking on the role of mom when our mother passed at a young age, and just being there for your children, grandchildren and great-grandchildren.

To my nieces, Kiyai and Janay—at just thirteen years old—you were my first editors. Thank you, for finding a missing word on the very first page of my manuscript. It let me know, no matter how many times you proofread your own work, you still need someone other than yourself to read it.

To my sister, Patrice Dorsey—"Patti Cakes"—and my brother-in-law, Arthur Betts, Jr.— "Artie"—thanks to you both for reading excerpts of my manuscript and offering some sound advice on certain passages. Your input made me look at my writing from another angle and incorporate some of your suggestions.

Thank-you for always being there and supporting me, Deidra, Shawn, Kenneth(Trish), Kalvin(Sherry), Keith(Natalie) and Karlton(Nicole), (my brother and sisters—the Dorsey's), Judy and Alan Davis (sister and brother in-law).

To my husband, Stephen, thank you for your continued encouragement in our discussions, for listening to my ideas about the book, for reading some paragraphs, and for emailing me helpful articles. I love you!

Thanks to my daughter, "Sherri Berri" and grandson, "Jalen Balen." Sherri, thank you for listening to me (endlessly) as I discussed my book, and for giving your coworkers excerpts of my book to read. Luv mommie dear!

Jalen, thank you for asking me on a regular basis, "Grandma when are you going to be finished with that book?" It propelled me to keep typing each day, week and month to follow through on this mission. Luv grandma!

About the Author

The author, Emerald Betts, is a CPA and business professional writing under the pen name "E. Marie". She lives with her family in Chicago, Illinois.

Mrs. Betts holds a Bachelor of Science degree in Accounting from the University of Illinois at Urbana-Champaign. She also holds a Master of Science degree in Communications from Northwestern University.

This is Emerald's first book publication.

Index

B
Bosses 61-74
Bullies 121-126

C
Car Pools 26
Childcare 27-28
Contributions 33-34
Cost of Living Allowance
    Increase 182
Credit Unions 25-26

D
Demotions 155-158
Dress Code 11-19

E
Email Etiquette 126
Employee Assistance Programs
    97-98
Exempt versus Non-Exempt
Employees 181-182

F
Firings 155-158
Friendships 37-38, 43-45
Fringe Benefits 29-32

G
Goal Setting 141-145
Golden Child or Kids 41-42
Gossip 95-96

H
Hidden Job Market 147-149

I
Internships 47-49

M
Mentors 47-48, 57-58

N
Networking 109-111, 147

O
Office Romance 39
Office Supplies or Tools
    21-23
Organizational Culture 55-56

P
Performance Reviews 85-91
Project Management 169-173
Promotions 177-182

R
Resume Update 151-152
Returning to School
141-145

S
Salary Increases 177-182
Savings Plans 31-32
Self Improvement 93-94
Sexual Harassment
127-131

T
Teamwork 106
Time Management 26, 99-106
Toxic Coworkers 43-45, 159-161
Transportation 25-26

V
Volunteering 33-34

W
Workspace 21

Bibliography

1. Phrase: "In order to avoid a war, you gotta prepare for it." – Read a similar phrase in a letter to the editor. Time Magazine (Years 2010-2011)

2. Credit Unions – Researched and verified information written via various Internet websites. (Years 2011-2013)

3. 403B and 401K Savings Plan – Researched and verified information written via various Internet websites. (Years 2011-2013)

4. Sexual Harassment – Researched and verified information written via various pamphlets and Internet websites. (Years 2011-2013)

5. Senate hearings on sexual harassment – Researched and verified information written via various Internet websites. (Years 2011-2013)

6. Quote: "Is it true? Is it kind? Is it necessary?" – Co-worker who gave me the quote: Van Marshall. (Years 2010-2011)

7. Exempt Versus Non-Exempt Employees – Researched and verified information written via various Internet websites. (Years 2011-2013)

8. Cost of Living Allowance – Researched and verified information written via various Internet websites. (Years 2011-2013)

9. Wikepedia – Researched or verified various definitions of certain words or phrases used in this book. (Years 2011-2014)

Made in the USA
Charleston, SC
07 October 2014